Creole Feast

Creole Feast:
15 Master Chefs of New Orleans Reveal Their Secrets

Nathaniel Burton and Rudy Lombard
University of New Orleans Press
Manufactured in the United States of America

ISBN: 9781608011506

Cover photograph by Thomas Price
Book and cover design by Alex Dimeff
Photographs of the chefs are courtesy of Frank Lotz Miller.
The photographs in the introduction are courtesy of Charles Bailey.

First edition 2020
Printed on acid-free paper

THE UNIVERSITY OF NEW ORLEANS PRESS
unopress.org

Creole Feast

fifteen master chefs of new orleans
reveal their secrets

NATHANIEL BURTON
RUDY LOMBARD

Recently I have found myself in a rather celebrated category, one that makes me wonder whether I have deserved the status that people in New Orleans have given me. Although I have put forth every effort to earn this reputation, I am reluctant to lay claim to it. I have tried my best to train cooks, and I have met with some success; but it is the individual who makes the difference. I hope this book will serve as a memorial to those I had the pleasure of teaching.

I have cooked for forty years and enjoyed the patronage of some of the most famous people in the world, but I am confident that my wife, Irene C. Burton, has been the inspiration for it all. Therefore I am happy to dedicate this book to her; she has always encouraged and cherished me, and my devotion to her is immeasurable.

NATHANIEL BURTON

I offer this dedication to Dolores and Warren Lombard, Essie Hobbs Smith, Nettie Minor, Berdis Baldwin, and Louise Burgen.

RUDY LOMBARD

ACKNOWLEDGMENTS

We wish to express our sincere thanks to our many friends whose assistance and generosity made the completion of this book possible. Special thanks to Roland and Edwin Lombard, Overton Perkins, Freddie Kohlman, Danny and Louise (Blue Lu) Barker, Melville Wolfson, Mr. and Mrs. Jack Nelson, Wayne Miller, and Lolis E. Elie.

For their help in providing photographs, materials, and pertinent information, we are indebted to Mrs. Leah Chase, Mr. and Mrs. Raymond Thomas, Marie Matthews, Mrs. Leroy Rhodes, Al Pierce, Marie Boon, James Plauche, and David Gooch. For the especially brilliant photographs of the chefs, we wish to thank Jean and Frank Lotz Miller.

Much of the hard work associated with this book rested on the energy, talent, dependability, and pleasant personality of Beverly A. Jackson, who transcribed and typed much of the manuscript. A special thanks to Marilyn Dowden and to Charlene Mays, who helped us over the rough spots.

For their continued support, encouragement, and love, a special expression of thanks is due James and Caryn Hobbs, Fletcher and Nadine Robinson, and Denise Nicholas.

In New Orleans, it is customary to end a gourmet experience on a sweet note, so we do that here by recognizing the invaluable assistance rendered by our "no-nonsense" editor, Toni Morrison. More than anything, this book is a reflection of her energy, patience, and commitment.

—N.B & R.L.

CONTENTS

MEATS

SAUCES AND DRESSINGS

EGG DISHES

FOREWORD FOR *CREOLE FEAST*
BY LEAH CHASE

In 1941, when I was eighteen years old, I had never been in a restaurant, and I had seldom cooked at home. But I got a job as a waitress in the French Quarter, and that's where I learned about the full diversity of New Orleans food. The restaurant did not have a freezer, so we had to wrap the meat up in paper and keep it down in the ice house. Whenever the chef needed more meat, I would go out and bring it back to the restaurant. I would go back into the kitchen, help wash the dishes, which you did by hand back then, and talk to the chef. I asked this big man, "Why don't you have any women in here?" He told me that women weren't strong enough to lift the pots. And I told him, "What are you talking about? Who do you think is hauling all these packages of meat up and down the street? This sister."

When I came to Dooky Chase Restaurant in 1946, I noticed that black people were only cooking *our food* at home. We were always proud of what we cooked because it tasted so good, and I thought why not give it a try, throwing in a little of what I had observed in the French Quarter. So I started putting gumbo on the menu. I started putting jambalaya on the menu. And you know what? I found out that everybody wanted to eat what we were making in our homes. Then I started to see restaurants putting our food on their menus. But nobody really knew who was in the back, stirring the pot.

When Rudy Lombard started coming to Dooky Chase, it was like looking at God because he guided me. He put me on the map when he started to take me out on the road with other black chefs. And when he came up with the idea for *Creole Feast*, I don't think anybody fully understood what he was trying to do. Rudy was as smart as a whip, and he had great vision. This book was more than recipes. It was more than a cookbook. It showed people who was really behind the doors of all these big restaurants in New Orleans. *Creole Feast* made you think about what we had done to make a difference in the city.

I think that is why this book needs to be back in print. I hope that younger generations will read *Creole Feast*, with pride and respect, and learn from it. I hope they will see how black chefs worked hard to make Creole cooking important. I hope they will see why it was important to open the doors to kitchens and show the world who is making the barbequed shrimp. I think you need to teach people how to look at one another. You need to teach people how they can help one another. I learned from everybody, from Rudy and the other chefs in this book. That is what life is all about. You not only learn, but you have to say where you learned it. You have to tell the world the names of those that helped you and taught you. Every time I think about these people, I think I better work. I better try and make a difference. I better do my best to pay the highest tribute to them. And food will help you through everything. Food will ease you through your troubles.

New Orleans, 2017

INTRODUCTION

It is difficult to arrive at a universally satisfying definition of Creole cuisine. All such attempts in the past have failed to achieve a consensus and have seldom been used twice; several key influences or individuals are always left out or changed. The one feature, however, that all previous definitions have in common is a curious effort to ascribe a secondary, lowly, or nonexistent role to the Black hand in the pot, in spite of the fact that everything that is unique about New Orleans culture—its food, music, architecture, carnivals, voodoo, and lifestyle—can be traced to that city's Black presence. Quiet as it is kept, it is this fact that is at the center of the "Creole controversy," just as it was the major focus of nineteenth-century writers who insisted that the descriptive term "Creole" could only be applied to persons of European descent, notwithstanding evidence to the contrary.

French, Spanish, Cajun, Italian—all these ethnic groups live in New Orleans, but they are not running the kitchens of the best restaurants in the city. The single, lasting characteristic of Creole cuisine is the Black element.

Black involvement in the New Orleans Creole cuisine is as old as gumbo and just as important. It is unfortunate that local attitudes toward racial matters have not allowed the contributions of Black people to this cuisine to achieve the kind of preeminence they deserve. Commentary on this subject has traditionally been lacking in good taste. The 1850s images of mammies, slaves, *marchand* ladies singing *"Bel calas tout chauds,"* pickaninny art, and the "beloved" but economically and socially slighted female domestic cook are still entrenched in the social history and cooking literature of today. The graphics and descriptive character of early cookbooks rarely mention Black men, except for an occasional hunter who went about bagging wild game for his master's table—a table that was frequently a resplendent example of Creole *haute cuisine*. Southern cookbooks, especially those on New Orleans cooking, are heavily inundated with irreverent and whimsical language about Blacks, while several of the popular older cookbooks simply omit any reference to Blacks in their descriptions of the origins and influences of Creole cuisine.

In the last two decades, general writing on New Orleans food has changed somewhat. The change is a modest one, and the paucity of positive images is still with us, but every now and then one comes across newspaper articles about a Black chef or cook. And a few are thanked in the acknowledgments sections of recent cookbooks for lending their editorial assistance. Such changes are welcome, and one hopes they will continue. Yet the role of the Black chef remains grossly underrated, and quite often references to it are patronizing. It is not uncommon to find Black chefs referred to by first name only, and it is frequently implied that they lack originality and come upon the creation of an original dish by accident rather than by inventiveness.

There are many lovable traditions in New Orleans that deserve to be kept intact. The city has a culture both rich and mysterious. Tourists have always flocked to New Orleans. The great restaurants of the city and their owners have garnered lavish and well-earned praise. The good reputation of the French, Spanish, and Cajun styles of cooking are rightfully established, and the praise it receives is truly deserved, but for those of us who live here, it is the Creole cuisine that is the aristocrat of all cuisines.

In this book we introduce the reader to an elite group of Black chefs and cooks who, in our opinion, make up the finest selection of Creole cooking talent in the world. All of them are professionals who have held or are at present holding top culinary positions in the most renowned and widely acclaimed restaurants in New Orleans. They are not "Creole" in the sense in which the term implies native-born. Most of them were not born in New Orleans, although practically all were reared there. They do not have typical Creole names derived from French and Spanish, nor do they speak the local Creole patois. Nevertheless, they are the masters of the New Orleans cuisine—it is because of them that it exists today, and they are the very best at what they do. Their cooking style encompasses a creative improvisation not unlike that found among traditional New Orleans Black jazz musicians. Their genius relies largely on experience, combined with the full use and development of all five senses. What they measure by touch tends to be as accurate as if measured by a scale or cooking instrument; what they hear while deep-frying tends to be as accurate a gauge as a timer; what they judge by sight and smell will more often than not satisfy the most discriminating taste. They do measure ingredients; not only with equipment but also with the cupped hands and the pinch of their fingertips.

The men and women who make up this prestigious circle of chefs are all primarily self-taught rather than formally trained. Almost without exception they began their professional careers as dishwashers. Along the way they received help, guidance, and assistance (were tutored, if you will) from other professionals who, like them, also lacked formal training. In this sense, they are proud heirs to the rich legacy of Creole cuisine they have inherited from Black professional cooks. And it is certainly to their credit that they have perfected the art of Creole cooking in almost complete anonymity and frequently in a hostile environment.

The senior chefs among those included here often talk for hours about the other Black chefs who were their peers and teachers. Their reminiscences reflect the great mutual respect and the enormous pride they take in their profession. As one of the senior chefs said, "To the chefs I worked with every order was important, and there was always an attempt to cook it to perfection; to make it something you could be proud of."

Those Black men and women of an earlier generation deserve special mention for their outstanding contribution to Creole cooking:

Chef Louis Bluestein (Brennan's, Roosevelt Hotel, Pontchartrain Hotel, Hotel New Orleans) was widely acclaimed and respected among his peers for his extraordinary versatility in all aspects of cooking. His stint as executive chef at Brennan's is legendary among his fellow chefs and friends, especially with regard to the preparation of egg dishes and sauces.

Leona Victor was for years a private cook at the home of the celebrated Corinne Dunbar, a supreme hostess who opened her famous restaurant on the strength of Mrs. Victor's ingenious cooking skills. Mrs. Victor created the famous Oysters and Artichokes Dunbar and Dunbar's Banana Beignet, as well as most of the other original recipes for which Dunbar's became noted. She was a Black Creole who spoke the patois and cooked without benefit of written recipes or formal training. *Mrs. Clara Mathus* succeeded Mrs. Victor and remained at Dunbar's for twenty-five years.

Mrs. Lena Richards was a culinary giant of her era with over thirty years of success as a caterer. In 1937, Mrs. Richards opened a cooking school and two years later published her famous *New Orleans Cookbook*. In 1947, she started the first and only television show in New Orleans featuring a Black cook.

Mrs. Christine Warren was highly successful as a caterer whose services were greatly prized by the wealthy white families of the city. She operated her business for more than thirty-five years, and was said to possess one of the finest collections of silverware in the city.

Other notable chefs include Charles Hall (Monteleone Hotel—twenty-five years); Isaac Harris (Commander's Palace, Brennan's, Broussard's, La Louisiane—forty years); Bob Richards (Commander's Palace—twenty-five years); and Dan Williams (Pontchartrain Hotel—fifteen years).

This list is partial and says nothing about the many Black chefs and cooks who brought distinction to their jobs in Pullman cars, merchant-marine galleys, cooking schools, and private homes. This book is a tribute to all of them, and it is our hope that the record is now somewhat straightened and that the masters of the Creole cuisine will become as well known as the cuisine itself. We hope you enjoy this fare, and as they say in New Orleans, let the *"bon temps roulette."*

R. J. L.

PART ONE:
THE CHEFS

NATHANIEL BURTON

Nathaniel Burton was born in McComb, Mississippi in 1914 and was one of nine children. He left Mississippi in 1939 and came to New Orleans, taking a job at the Hotel New Orleans on Canal Street as a bushoy. He graduated to washing glasses and then to washing dishes. He had no idea what the food industry was all about, so he began watching the chef he worked for, Dan Williams, very carefully. Williams's help, and the knowledge gained from reading every book he could find, including a Creole cookbook published by the Times Picayune *and* Escoffier *(which he memorized), prepared him for a brilliant career as a chef. He cooked in many places after leaving the Hotel New Orleans, including the Pontchartrain Hotel and Broussard's. He left the latter in the forties to handle the cooking at the Navy hospital, where he supervised some one hundred and sixty employees, serving from three to five thousand people. He received a citation for his work there from the Undersecretary of the Navy, James Forrestal, in 1943. Mr. Burton, who is now executive chef at Broussard's, has had a career that has spanned teaching apprentice cooks from the Culinary Institute in Hyde Park, New York, lectures and demonstrations at Cornell University Hotel School, building up a clientele in several restaurants, and maintaining a dedicated following of gourmets throughout the years. Some of these include Mary Martin, Joshua Logan, Tony Randall, Craig Claiborne, Duke Ellington, Louis Armstrong, Joseph Cotton, Kay Ballard, Charles Laughton, Walt Disney, Amy Vanderbilt, Sammy Davis Jr., Dr. Milton Eisenhower, Duncan Hines, "Bear" Bryant, and Franklin Roosevelt, Jr.*

The outstanding characteristic of a chef is dedication and a willingness to work. The average cook works eight hours and has completed his day, but the exceptional chef works ten hours, twelve hours, fifteen hours if necessary to get the job done. And

even after working that length of time, he's not tired; he enjoys
his work and perhaps it takes that long to accomplish what he
set out to do for that particular day.

The talents I look for in an exceptional chef are many. He
should be well-versed in all the fundamentals of cooking, and
he should have thorough knowledge of meats. Once the meat
has been butchered, a piece of veal, beef, or whatever, he should
be able to identify it. If there's a single piece of round or chuck
lying on the board, he should know precisely what it is, even
if no other part of the meat is near. The same thing applied to
various fowl. He should know the difference between a duck, a
guinea fowl, a quail, a pheasant, a Cornish hen, whatever, and
be able to identify precisely what it is. Above all, he should be
knowledgeable about seafood. He should be able to look at a fish
tenderloin and know exactly what kind of fish it is, whether it is
trout, redfish, red snapper, pompano, a grouper, or a croaker; he
should be able to go right through the list and immediately say,
"This is trout, this is redfish, this is red snapper." He should also
master the fundamental processes of cooking: frying, roasting,
baking, sautéing, broiling. He should know the exact difference
between each type of cooking, and he should be able to do them
all. He should know his tools, the utensils that are used in the
kitchen, what they're good for and what they do to food. When
the Culinary Institute in Hyde Park sends students to serve
apprenticeships with us, we have to give them expert kitchen
experience. Sometimes these students will arrive not knowing
the difference between a strip loin and a tenderloin. An apprentice might not know how to select or purchase the pots he will
need in his business.

A chef should also be able to create dishes when he's in
a pinch. I think this is one of the greatest and most difficult
tests of a really first-rate chef. Some of the dishes we are consistently asked to prepare, and which have now become standards
in New Orleans, are dishes that have come about under such

circumstances. Sometimes you'll have a customer, a regular customer, who is fastidious and comes in with an uncertain appetite, knowing only that he wants something in the seafood line, for example, but doesn't know exactly what. The Shrimp and Oyster Brochette was developed that way, so were the Oysters Caribbean. I was really trying to make another dish at the time, but I was swamped with work and I didn't want him to wait too long. So I decided to grill the oysters, put a little green onion in them, and add some cream sauce, beef stock, and a dash of Worcestershire sauce. I casseroled it and sent it to him. He never questioned it, and he and his guests loved it. And ever since then, we've had Oysters Caribbean and a huge clientele eating them. The Steak à la Burton is a sirloin strip that I developed pretty much on the spur of the moment. The same thing is true of the Redfish Court Bouillon. That was a dish I prepared for the Food and Wine Society of New York at their dinner party at the Harvard Club in New York. Trying to find something different for another party, I came up with the Crêpe Soufflé and another time with the Stuffed Eggplant with Oysters.

Experimenting, trying to develop new and tasty recipes, and being able to produce something fine under duress—all these are characteristics of chefs I admire.

Although most of what I am saying is applicable to hotel and restaurant chefs only, the same kind of spontaneous creation and the ability to build on foods already in the kitchen are important to any good cook. In a home kitchen, you have to be able to identify good food. I have worked in restaurants where the business has fallen off and where I've taken two weeks to find out what went wrong. At one place I remember they were using an inferior potato. The best baked potato on the market is the Idaho Russet U.S. #1. I also had to make sure that all the seafood was fresh. One of the worst things you can do in a kitchen or in a restaurant is to serve a bad piece of seafood. You can have five hundred orders of fresh seafood, and two bad pieces will ruin you because you get more publicity from two bad pieces than you get from five hundred good ones. So you do anything in the world to prevent that.

Also, you have to be able to make all the soups from scratch. No canned soups. And the consistency of the food is of vital importance. Here in New Orleans, the cooking is as distinctive as it is in any part of the country. We probably use more seasoning than they do elsewhere. One of our native seasonings is bay leaf. Bay grows plentifully here in Louisiana, and we can get the leaves fresh and green—they are much more preferable in cooking than the dried ones. Dried bay leaves simply don't have the flavor that the fresh ones have, and you have to use much more in order to get the flavor.

Another seasoning popular in New Orleans is thyme, which is grown here and is heavily used in Creole food. Chives is another one. There are both wild and cultivated chives. The cultivated chives don't have the flavor that the wild chives do and don't mix with food in precisely the same way. When people want baked potato with sour cream and chives, there's a distinct difference between the potato in which wild chives are used and the one in which cultivated chives are used. Creole cooking is strongly influenced by Italian, Spanish, French, Chinese, and other cuisines, and from them we get not only our heavy use of oregano, sweet basil, and marjoram but also some excellent sauces. Good sauce is pretty much the essence of good cooking.

There are four basic sauces, which we call universal sauces. They are brown sauce, red sauce, white sauce, and hollandaise sauce. Every one of those sauces with the exception of hollandaise can be prepared and stored. And if you're doing Creole cooking consistently, that's precisely what one should do. It takes a long time to prepare the red, the brown, or the white sauce, and you should make it in large quantities and store it in the refrigerator, using the smaller portions as you need them for each dish. When you put the sauce in the refrigerator, it will collect a layer of cooled fat on top. You should let the fat stay on because it serves as a protective coat, and you can keep the sauce quite fresh so long as you don't break the fat up. You can keep it for two or three weeks if your refrigerator is around thirty-five to forty degrees.

When you want a Marchand de Vin sauce, which includes finely chopped and sliced mushrooms, you would add beef marinade and red wine to the brown sauce. And since the brown sauce takes so long to prepare, at least thirty-five to forty minutes just to get the roux ready, you would want to have it available to you immediately when making any sauce the basic ingredient of which is a brown sauce. Making the beef stock that goes in a brown gravy is in itself a long preparation. You take beef bones and veal bones and brown them in an oven. Then put them in a pot and cover them with water. You also have to brown the vegetables you put in there—onions, garlic, celery, carrots—and once that is cooked thoroughly, you have to strain it. It will be a light brown color once you finish with it, and you pour it into the roux. The roux is flour and shortening blended together, and it has to be stirred constantly in order to get an even brown color and an excellent nutty flavor. These two elements, the stock and the roux, will produce a good brown sauce.

Another thing that is important in good cooking is learning how to save food, how not to waste it, and how to use the leftovers to the best advantage. Sometimes you cook more link sausages than you need, and it may appear that those that are not served are wasted because they shrivel. Actually, if you put a little water over them, they plump right up and you can use them again. The same thing applies to French bread. There is a thing in New Orleans called "lost bread," which simply means stale bread. There are any number of recipes that incorporate the use of so-called lost bread. You learn that if you put mushrooms in a refrigerator along with other kinds of food, the mushrooms will cause the other foods to mold faster than if the mushrooms were not in the refrigerator at all. So mushrooms should always be stored separately.

You have to learn where the flavoring is coming from in many of your dishes so that you won't throw valuable parts away. The head of a fish, for example, is where the best flavor is in a court bouillon. Many people throw the head away, but if you use the head for the stock, the flavor produced is tremendous—one you can't get anywhere else. You have to learn which seafood goes with which soup. Redfish is best for the court bouillon. Snapper is better for broiling, and it's excellent for poaching. Other fish doesn't do well poached.

It's an intriguing business, cooking. And it never ceases to excite or challenge me. I love the preparation and serving of excellent food. Although I have to admit that my favorite dish is one my mother used to make. She could take those small new potatoes and add salt meat and onions to them. I don't do anything that tasted that good. You could sit down at the table and just eat those potatoes. And you know, I never found out exactly how she cooked them.

RAYMOND THOMAS, SR.

Raymond Thomas, Sr. started in the restaurant business in 1934 as a dishwasher. He has cooked at Commander's Palace, T. Pittari's, and Brennan's. He is now head chef at the French Market Seafood House, which is famous for its Crabmeat Lafitte, Trout Gresham, gumbo, and turtle soup. It is clear from the recipes he describes and his recollections of the men he knew who prepared them that he loves the beautiful work of a cook.

I like making okra gumbo. When I prepare it, I cook my seasonings on the side, not in the pot. I make a roux and a fish stock, add shrimp, crabs, and all the other meats. The okra I put in at the very last. I cook the okra in butter by itself. That way I know the okra will come out tender, and it won't burn or scorch as much as it would if I cooked it in oil. Then I drain the butter off before adding it to the gumbo. Cooking the okra this way cuts down on the sticky juice that okra produces. When I make gumbo at home, I cut the crabs in half and leave them in the shell. That way, the flavor is kept in. In restaurant cooking, we take the shell off because a customer might get a piece of shell in his throat, and many people don't like to see food in its natural state. But home-style gumbo is different from restaurant gumbo and tastes better, too. You can put in chicken feet, chicken backs, crabs in the shell, the little crab paws, and you don't have to strain the seasoning. After it sits for two or three days, it is at the peak of its flavor. That's when gumbo is really gumbo. But I never put oysters in gumbo. I know a lot of people do, but if you put oysters in and it sits in the refrigerator a day or two (as it should to be really good), the oysters will sour the gumbo. If somebody wants oysters, add them just before serving. The same thing is true of other soups. Vegetable soup, turtle soup, even oyster soup will keep a week in the refrigerator. It won't spoil or turn sour there because it doesn't have any tomatoes in it. The acid in the tomatoes seems to eat at any oyster and sour it. But in oyster soup there is just the oyster, green onions, roux, oyster water, salt, and pepper. Seasonings have a tendency to cook the oysters in a gumbo and make it foamy—then you have lost your gumbo.

Also, I prefer green onions to chives. Chives are dry and strong. Green onions can be cut up to look like chives, but they bring out a flavor nicely, whereas chives can produce a bitter taste.

In making the roux, I use oil instead of butter, and I use my own judgment about the amounts. When my cooking oil is hot, I drop in the plain flour—I have my whisk ready, and I begin to stir it to knock the lumps out. But if the roux is needed for the cream sauce on certain seafood dishes, you need a buttery taste—with the Crabmeat au Gratin, for instance—then I use half butter and half oil. Then when the color is right, I add milk.

I always use fresh seasonings. I'll use a whole "paw" or bulb of garlic, for example, in certain recipes. Garlic purée is just a name—it has no flavor. Of course cooking with fresh seasonings takes longer, but that's my way. I even use fresh green beans.

If you are making a gumbo at home, you don't serve it just after it has finished cooking. You remove it from the stove and let it cool. Take the cover off just a little, not all the way off, just enough to let the air hit. It can sit there up to five hours, but if you are not serving for five or more hours, put it in the refrigerator and warm it up when you are about to use it. If you have made a big pot of gumbo, just remove from it the portion you want to serve—don't keep heating and reheating the whole pot.

When I choose trout, I prefer a small one. Three pounds is good enough. When they are too big, you have to cook them to death. The smaller ones you can cook quickly and not cook the flavor out. I buy all my fish whole, and I freeze them whole. Never clean a fish and freeze it. Don't take the head off or remove the entrails. When it's thawed, it's a fresh fish again. Everybody buys trout fillet, redfish fillet—all sorts of filleted fish—but once you freeze a fillet, when you take it out and thaw it for cooking, you'll find that all of its flavor is gone. When you freeze a whole fish, don't cover it or anything. Leave the gills and everything on, and it will keep six to eight months in the freezer and be as fresh as the sea when you take it out. That's because it's the entrails that give it the flavor and sustain the flavor. A filleted fish will keep its flavor about twenty-four hours, and then the flavor is gone.

The backbone of the fish is where the best of its meat is. The head, too. Both parts are vital in the making of a court bouillon. I never throw any fish bones away.

In making stock, a beef stock for example, put the shell of an egg in the pot along with the beef, onions, peppers, and so on. The eggshell will float on top and clear the stock. Otherwise, you will have to filter it through filtering paper if you want it to be a clear stock. The eggshell will bring the fat and the scum from the meat to the top, and you can skim it off.

I've worked with some of the greatest chefs there are. Louis Bluestein specialized in eggs. People came from all over for his omelets. He created an artichoke omelet—a very difficult thing to do because, you know, artichokes hold water, and water and eggs and butter will stick to a pan. But Louis could roll this artichoke omelet so beautifully; it looked just like a pie, each end barely touching the edge of the plate. I never found out how he kept it from sticking. It was some way he had of putting the oil in the pan. When Louis made hollandaise sauce, he never used a double boiler; he cooked it on an open flame, directly on the fire, and when he got all of his eggs, margarine (he would never use butter), lemons, Tabasco sauce, salt, and pepper, he would start to work and hand-beat it for about an hour. He handled the flame in such a way that the sauce would not break, and he never changed his stroke. Once I asked him why didn't he whip it the other way. He said if he changed his stroke he would have to start all over again.

Then there was James Evans at Commander's Palace. He created a Bienville sauce that became famous. And to make the sauce, he never used fish stock. He boiled shrimp but didn't use the water from them. He made his own stock with milk. And he made a turtle stew that had everybody running there to buy it. He used a soft turtle shell for stewing, and he put absinthe in his roux. His assistant, Bob Richardson, made a meat loaf we called "Bob's Glorified Meat Loaf." He had a way of taking one green pepper and cutting it oblong. Then he took pimento and put that under it, and he'd roll it. When the meat loaf came out and was sliced, you would see three or four bouquets of color in each slice. He made a cream soup that never curdled. It was a beautiful golden color, which he got by whipping three egg yolks and some half-and-half for about five minutes. He added that to the cream soup just before he took it off the stove. He could slice asparagus into triangles for his asparagus soup, and when you spooned it up, you always got two or three pieces—and it held and would never break up.

Joe Hawkins could broil any meat: steak, veal. He manipulated the flame—just the flame—in such a way that every meat he broiled came out tender. Sometimes we would deliberately give him a particularly tough piece of meat to broil. When he got through with it, it was soft as butter. He never put anything on the meat to make it tender; he just used the fire in a special way.

Those old chefs loved cooking, and they were dedicated to it. They were beautiful. Even the waiters were proud of them. They knew good cooking takes time, and if the customer was restless, they would just calm him, ask him if he wanted another drink. The food couldn't be sacrificed for anybody. When a chef is preparing a meal, he feels like it's his own.

LEAH CHASE

Leah Chase is co-owner of the famous Dooky Chase Restaurant, which Ray Charles made even more famous in the song "Early in the Morning": "I went to Dooky Chase/To get something to eat/ The waitress looked at me and said,/'Ray, you sure look beat'/Now it's early in the morning,/And I ain't got nothing but the blues." Mrs. Chase cooked at home with her mother and sisters—all excellent cooks—before coming to Dooky Chase, where she learned the specialties of Creole cuisine, particularly the art of serving and cooking with wine. Her father made the best strawberry wine— from vine-ripened berries—she can remember. The restaurant is a family business that began as a lunch counter run by her father- and mother-in-law, the original Mr. and Mrs. Dooky Chase. Now she handles this landmark among New Orleans restaurants.

I like what thyme does to things. It really gives certain foods a special taste. I don't think anybody is really cooking red beans, for instance, unless they put a little thyme in them and some bay leaf. In my gumbo, I put thyme and one other important thing— paprika. Now if you make gumbo in too large a quantity, you don't get the best taste. If the pot's too big, the flavor will die a little. I put stew meat in mine. Veal is used a lot in some places, but I think it's too light with the two kinds of sausages and the ham. Some people think of gumbo with only fish or only meat. But here in the South, every cook puts a variety of things in the gumbo.

For my gumbo, I don't buy the filé powder off the shelves. My daddy makes it for me. He grinds it himself, and it is perfect because it is pure sassafras. He has sassafras trees, and he dries the leaves. The filé from a store will have maybe a little bay leaf in it, and it's much weaker. Mine is pure sassafras, nothing mixed in, and it's always fresh and strong. Daddy sends it to me in little mayonnaise bottles.

One of the most important items in Creole cooking is the roux. And the most important thing about making a roux is to stick with it. A good cook stays with the pots. You can't put certain foods on the stove and leave them. I use vegetable oil for my roux. Lard is best, just as lard is best for biscuits. In a restaurant, it doesn't work out because it burns too fast and requires too much attention. But peanut oil gives a taste that is almost as good as lard. Peanut oil has a flavor that is different and holds up better than the other shortenings or other oils. The second thing is to fry the flour properly. When you make a roux and you don't fry the flour really well, you get what Creoles call *Cata Plac*, and that isn't a good gravy. It is gooey—what we call a long gravy. You have to stay right there to get it just the right color. I like my roux a little golden, so I add paprika. I never use an artificial caramel coloring. I want my roux to look the same and taste the same all the time. When I start a gumbo pot, I don't leave it until it's done and just simmering. If you don't have time to cook, I think you should just get a sandwich.

But if you have to get a sandwich, the best one around is hot sausage on French bread. The next is oysters over pork chops on French bread. You can't beat that for a sandwich. And of course the pan-bread sandwiches. I wish I could make those for the restaurant, but they are so expensive to make, and I would have to charge a lot. But believe me, they are delicious.

ANNIE LAURA SQUALLS

Annie Laura Squalls started cooking professionally in 1949. First as a salad girl, then a pastry cook at the Meal-a-Minute. In 1954, she went to the Bienville. When that restaurant closed in 1960, she went to the Pontchartrain Hotel, and in her twenty-five years as head baker, she has continued her highly creative manipulation of practically every recipe given to her. Her breads, pastries, and desserts are so much in demand that once when she had to take care of her sick mother, the bakery section of the Pontchartrain almost closed down. No one could duplicate her expertise. As Chef Louis Evans says, "What Annie Laura doesn't know about pastry, nobody knows about pastry."

I always have to figure out how I really want a dish to be. If I don't like the way a recipe sounds, I just change it. It all started from the time I was asked to cook things I'd never cooked in my life, and I had to think it through carefully. A cherry cobbler, for instance. When I was first asked to make one, I was confused. I had no idea how to do it. So I started out by draining the cherries and cooking the juice. Then I wanted some thickening that wouldn't make the pie gummy. I knew cornstarch was the usual ingredient, but I thought that cornstarch alone was too much. I added flour to it—half as much flour as cornstarch. I cooked it into the juice and added the cherries. I mixed it and let it all cook a little while. Then I thought I'd add lemon juice, but I was not sure it would work because lemon juice is such a dominant flavoring. I put the cherries aside to cool before I added the juice, then I wondered what spices ought to go in. I decided on cinnamon because I thought I couldn't lose with that—and it turned out that the lemon juice, cinnamon, and sugar gave the pie a lovely taste. There were a lot of compliments.

I had no experience to speak of when I started, so I had to work out a recipe in my mind first. I think a good cook ought to do that anyhow, but I had a problem doing it in a restaurant because if I made up my own recipe, nobody could duplicate it. If I wasn't there, they were in trouble, and in a restaurant, consistency is important. So I started scribbling it all down. But I still had ideas about the food I was assigned to cook, and every time, it seemed, I'd change the recipe they gave me or the one in the cookbook I used. And I wouldn't tell anybody—I'd just change it, and if anybody asked me, I'd insist the recipe was the same. I didn't want anybody to be angry with me for not using the recipe I was given. Even when I cook ordinary food at home, I have to do it my way. I like food to blend well with the seasoning. I guess you could say I cook only for myself.

When I was asked to make sweet rolls by the owner of this restaurant, I heard the "sweet" part, and I didn't like the recipe he gave me. I started using a Danish pastry dough. It seemed to me the rolls needed a little icing. The owner didn't like icing on them, so I asked him about it and he said, "Try a little molasses." I thought, Molasses? Well, I took a little dark Karo syrup and chopped some pecans up fine with some sugar and grated lemon peel and brushed that on top of the dough. They loved it, but they still think it's molasses I brush it with.

When I started doing apple pies at the Pontchartrain Hotel, I sneaked a little vanilla and lemon juice into them while the head baker was away. It wasn't in the recipe they gave me, and I promised not to do it again, but when I had to do the orange cake, I sneaked grated orange rind into the icing. Just the orange flavoring alone wasn't enough for me. The same thing happened with the mile-high ice cream pie. They were accustomed to making it with two flavors of ice cream—chocolate and vanilla. I didn't like the way it looked—it wasn't colorful enough. There was too much white, what with the vanilla and the meringue. So I added strawberry. I also used more egg whites than the recipe called for, to make the meringue higher. I wanted it sweeter, too, so I added more sugar. I tried to stay in good with the cooks and the pantry so I could get a little extra cream or butter. When I worked with Mr. Burton at the Caribbean Room, he'd let me have a little extra sometimes, but frequently I'd wait until his back was turned and pilfer it.

I make an old-fashioned bread pudding with regular bread, not French. But it has to be stale bread. If you don't have stale bread, put fresh bread in the oven, dry it out, then butter it like toast when you take it from the oven. Then cut it up into pieces. I add apples diced very fine, fresh coconut, and crushed pineapple. If you can't get fresh coconut, use the canned. It's fresher-tasting than the kind that comes in a bag. Drain the pineapple because if you don't, the pudding will be soggy. Vanilla sauce goes nicely with it.

After the holidays, Christmas and Thanksgiving, mincemeat is sometimes left over. I suggested using it to make mincemeat turnovers. I chop an apple into the mincemeat to cut that too-spicy taste, and I roll it into the pastry dough and pinch it together to make a rectangle. I prick the crust with a fork and top the turnover with brandy sauce.

When most people make biscuits they have either too much shortening or too little. I started putting half butter and half vegetable shortening in my biscuit dough. They stay fresher and softer much longer that way. You have to cream the butter first at room temperature. And I put a little sugar in my baking powder and salt mixture. Because so much of the success of biscuits is in the blending—you can handle it too much—I solved the problem by putting the dry ingredients in the bowl, mounding it up into a hill; then I put the shortening and the butter in the middle with the milk. When the shortening is in the center like that, you can work it up quickly and lightly from the sides. It will cut down on the handling and keep your biscuits from coming out hard.

For the shortcake in strawberry shortcake, I don't like the biscuits sliced in half. It's like hardtack—too hard to eat and too hard to handle at the table. So I make a not-too-rich batter like cake batter.

There are lots of little things you learn as you go along: Sugar in pancakes made from scratch makes them brown better. Strain any cooked sauce that has egg in it because the eggs have a way of cooking up into bits and pieces. If you are making an icing, a pinch of cream of tartar helps to harden it; it also helps to thicken egg white for a meringue. When I make sweet potato turnovers, I add whiskey to the filling. And when you cream butter and sugar for a cake batter, mix the butter and sugar so well that you don't see a single grain of sugar. It should be remembered that for baking purposes, ingredients such as milk, eggs, cream cheese, and so forth are best used at room temperature.

LOUIS EVANS

Chef Louis Evans was born into a family of eight children in Carlisle, Mississippi. Following a family move, he completed his high school education in New Orleans and entered a local vocational college, where he studied cooking. In 1959, he accepted a position as a cook in a suburban New Orleans restaurant, working closely with Dorothy Montgomery, one of the city's finest culinary artists. He attended the Louisiana Vocational and Technical School's culinary arts program, supplementing his academic training with work as a cook. In 1961, he was promoted to the position of head chef in the restaurant in which he had first worked. He remained there until 1969, when he joined the staff of the Pontchartrain Hotel. In 1973, Louis Evans assumed the responsibility of executive chef at that hotel and has since been recognized among his peers, both locally and internationally, as one of New Orleans's most talented chefs.

I'm an old-fashioned cook. I don't believe in short cuts. To be a good cook, you need more than a school. A school can only teach you so much, and it can only give you a grade. What's needed is pride. I've worked for the best cooks there are, and all of them had that fierce pride about what they were doing in the kitchen. When I was at the Pontchartrain in the beginning, I worked for Mr. Burton, the head chef there, as his assistant. When he left, I was offered that job, but I refused it. I didn't think I was as good as Mr. Burton. They gave the job to a Frenchman, and I went on vacation. Six months after they hired the Frenchman, he was gone. They called me and offered the job to me again. I took it, but I never relaxed. That is a mistake some executive chefs make—they have the title, and they begin to try and cook from the office. If you stay in the office and not in your kitchen, some man out there on the line can cut your throat, professionally. A good chef has to do two things: be able to put anything in a pot and cook it right, and be able to supervise. You yourself have to be able to do the job you are telling somebody else to do. The excitement of it is getting into it, working the line. If you see somebody make a mistake, you have to be able to fix it right then and there so it will go out to the customer like it's supposed to. You can rework a recipe many ways in a crisis. Flour, for example, has a tendency to break down in some recipes, even when you use the same amount as before. Sometimes the flour has too much water in it, and it won't tighten up. If you're right there to direct, you can save it.

I enjoy the pantry, being behind the lines, sautéing, broiling, making salads, baking—all of it. And I'm always in and out of my icebox. I want to know what's in there. I don't take anybody's word for what supplies there are.

One of the best parts of this business is creating recipes and trying to improve on them. I made an oyster and artichoke soup that's a standard here now.

I created Shrimp 21. This dish is similar to Shrimp Newburg, but I boil the shrimp until they are half cooked, and then I sauté mushrooms to put in the roux. I add the stock to the shrimp, some sherry, some Sauterne, and blend it all together. Then I add salt and pepper. I let it cook down while I make a light pastry shell with regular pastry dough. When the shell is done, I put the shrimp mixture in it and serve it with fresh asparagus. Use fresh seasonings whenever you can. The most inferior seasonings are the dried ones. It takes a lot of tasting to get the flavor right if you use them because they have lost a lot of their original strength.

For Trout Véronique, I use tenderloin of speckled trout and white grapes.

For the hollandaise sauce, I prefer tarragon vinegar to lemon juice. It doesn't come up as fast with lemon juice. And when you heat a dish that is covered with hollandaise sauce, don't leave it in the oven over five minutes, or it will separate. Three minutes under a broiler is preferable. A poached trout with wine over it should not be put in too hot an oven—450° is fine.

The problem with some of the new cooks is that they are only used to cooking with portioned food. I don't believe in portion controls. You give a side of veal and a knife to some of the young cooks these days, and they don't know what to do. Or they will cook a fish without even knowing what kind of fish it is. You hear of cooks who hide their recipes—they won't ever tell you what's in them. And they hide their little tricks, too. Those are scared cooks. They are scared somebody will take their job or do a recipe just as well as they do and they'll lose the credit they have. A first-rate chef will tell you everything he does. He's not scared; he knows he's good and can compete with anybody. And he knows that if you're a second-rate cook, all the details in the world won't make you a first-rate one.

It's easy to make mistakes in cooking if you don't think about what you are doing or if you just stay with the cookbook. Many people don't realize it, but there is such a thing as a raw roux. Some people don't cook it enough. They just pour the hot liquid and the cold flour into the pot. They think if it cooks long enough it will taste the same as if you have browned the flour first. No way. You have to cook a roux slowly until it cooks all the way down. You'll know it's done when it gets to be the color you really want it to be—a lovely brown. I can tell when it's done by the smell and the flavor.

Two important things to remember about cooking are taking pride in your work and not being afraid to experiment. Once you know what you can do with food, you can trust yourself. I love it. Give me something to cook and some fire—and that's it.

AUSTIN LESLIE

Austin Leslie began cooking at Portia's Fountain on South Rampart Street. He left there in 1952 and went to Washington, D.C., where he cooked for a year in a Hot Shoppes while he attended business school. Homesick for his native New Orleans, he left Washington in 1953 and returned to Portia's. Two years later, he quit to work in a sheet-metal shop. When work was slow, he helped his aunt, who owned a small restaurant on Perdido Street. In 1964, after a short stint at D. H. Holmes Restaurant, he opened his own place— Chez Hélène. It quickly became a favorite among tourists as well as native New Orleanians and remains one of the finest family restaurants in the city.

The first time I cut up a chicken, I was working at Portia's. The chef there, Bill Turner, asked me where I learned how to do it. I said I learned from my mother at home. He taught me how to get twelve pieces from a whole chicken; my mother was able to get thirteen pieces from the same chicken because she broke the back into two parts. I learned all about fried chicken from Bill Turner, too. It's the easiest job in the kitchen. You can tell by the sound when fried chicken is done. If you listen to it, you can hear how the sound of the grease crackling in the fryer changes. Then you know it's time to bring it up. I never cook it well done; I never cook any meat well done. What I do is take the blood out of it first—while the chicken is frying, take a pair of tongs and squeeze each piece. Squeeze it till it bursts to let the blood out. You can look right down there by the bone and see if there is any blood there. When it's ready, the chicken will float to the top, a part of it will stick up. Then you take it and check it over. If you cook it properly, you can keep your guests or customers from ever seeing any blood. That's what they object to when they prefer well-done meat—not the taste but the blood.

If you're serving fried chicken to twelve people, you will need three chickens so you can provide three pieces each. The wings —two pieces; the breast—four pieces; the back—two pieces; the thighs—two pieces; the legs—two pieces: That's twelve in all. Since people want to be able to handle chicken easily when they eat it, we cut it that way. Actually we can fry it just as well in larger cuts. When you cut it up properly, you won't loosen the skin. You start by cutting it from the back. Split it down the middle. Then take a sharp cleaver and place the chicken firmly on a block and hold it down. After you split it down the back, then you open it up and take out the insides and put them aside. Then you cut straight through the breast. Cut it into quarters with the cleaver, separating the thighs from the breast. Then disjoint it at the wings, and disjoint the legs from the thighs. If you use a cleaver, be careful. If you use a knife, always cut away from yourself. Always move all other knives away from the board when you use a cleaver because you can misstrike, and if that cleaver hits a knife, it can jump up and hit you.

After the chicken is cut up, salt and pepper it, mixing the pieces around so the salt and pepper get all over the chicken.

If you are preparing the chicken to be cooked later, don't do what they do in markets—cover it with plastic or wax paper. If you do that and then put it in the refrigerator, some of it might go bad. The best thing is to put the seasoned chicken in a bowl uncovered. That way the cold air can get all around the chicken and keep it fresh.

The next step is to make an egg wash. Use any kind of cream —for one chicken use one egg and half a can of evaporated milk.

Add some salt and pepper, stir it up, put the chicken in and let it sit. Put enough flour to cover the chicken either in a bag or in a flat bowl and coat the chicken with flour. If you use an electric fryer, set it to 350°; if you pan-fry, wait till the oil is beginning to bubble. I use peanut oil for frying. Put the heavy pieces in first (thigh, leg, and breast), making sure you don't crowd the chicken. If you put too much in at one time, the heat and oil can't get all around the meat, and it will cook unevenly. You have to watch the flour that falls to the bottom of the pan very carefully. After each set of pieces gets done, strain the oil out and clean the pan, otherwise the flour at the bottom is going to burn. You've heard people say the first chicken looks good, the second so-so, and the third you can forget. That's why. Never fry anything else (meat, fish, or sausage) along with the chicken because it will give it a bad taste. It's like frying hot sausage on a grill and then following it up with steak or ham. You see that a lot in restaurant kitchens, and that's why the food has such a strange taste. You can't cut up a lobster on the same board you use for chicken or some other meat.

For stewed chicken, I use hens. I parboil the hens to tenderize them. Put the cut-up chicken in water and boil for about an hour. Add onion, celery, salt, and pepper, and when it simmers down and cools off, skim the grease from the top for the brown gravy. Dice up parsley, onion, and celery and fry it lightly in the grease you've taken from the stewing chicken. That's how you get the chicken flavor in the gravy. Then you put the flour in the fryer and let it burn. Let it burn, burn, burn until it's brown enough. Really brown. Then add the juice from the broth the chicken was stewed in. Let it cook down. Then add the heavy pieces of chicken to the gravy, followed by the lighter pieces. Let it cook for about two or three hours. Check on it all the time because you don't want the meat falling off of the bones.

I never cover my pots because I have to look at the food I am cooking. If your pot is covered, you can't see what's going on. To be a successful cook you to have to take tender care and watch it. You can't leave it and go talk on the telephone. You can't leave your pots; you can't put food in a slow fryer and go downtown. You have to stay with it.

The old-fashioned way to make potato salad was to cook the potatoes whole. After they had cooked, you'd wash them off. Let them cool and then take the skin off. But it takes a lot of time to do it that way. For potato salad, I use twelve to fifteen large Idaho potatoes. They are better than the red ones. I use onions in potato salad only at home. In a restaurant I don't because when the salad is refrigerated with an onion in it, the acid of the onion gives it a bad odor. Customers will say it's sour, but it's only the onion's acid and the refrigeration taste. At home, the salad doesn't sit around, so you can use onion. Don't put any potato salad in the refrigerator until the hot potatoes cool off. If you do, it will stiffen up. Leave it until it's room temperature and then refrigerate it. But there are other foods that should go in the refrigerator hot. Hot food cools faster than cool food. If you want ice water fast, you put hot water in the pitcher; it will get colder quicker than room-temperature water will. If you want ice cubes fast, you put hot water in the tray. Food spoils faster if it's put in the refrigerator after it has hit room temperature. The best thing is to put it in straight from the stove.

When I bake yams, I put them in the oven and let them stay there until they explode. Then you take them out, peel them, and put them in an ovenproof dish with lemon juice and sugar. Put them back in the oven and let them simmer down. The best, of course, are fresh yams. In fact, fresh produce is always best. When I cook greens or cabbage, I prepare them a day ahead. I clean them and cut them up and soak overnight or longer with ice cubes right on top. That makes them tender.

For stuffed peppers, ten servings: You need a pound of peeled and deveined shrimp—I prefer the small shrimp for the pepper stuffing. Also a pound of ground meat, mostly beef, although some people like veal. Use a whole onion, celery, parsley, garlic, and dice it all up. Add it to a frying pan with a quarter of a stick of margarine (not butter, margarine). Sauté it and let it simmer down. Then take some stale French bread and break it up and wet it just enough to dampen it, not soak it, so you can handle it as though it were meatballs. Add it to the sautéed ingredients and then add about six eggs and a tiny piece of fresh garlic—not too much. Then you stir it all up and bake it for about one and a half hours. Then take it out and stir it again and let it stiffen. Put the dressing in the refrigerator to cool because you can't handle it hot, and you can get more dressing in the pepper if it's cold. Then halve your peppers from the side, not the top. You can parboil the peppers first if you like. After you cool the stuffing, the grease will solidify at the top. Scoop it off. Stuff the pepper and sprinkle breadcrumbs on top. To serve, put a little margarine or some of the same grease you scooped off and put it on top, then put the peppers in the broiler for ten to twelve minutes. But don't stand there and let them burn.

To boil shrimp, you do the same thing you do with lobster: season your water first. Let the water come to a boil with the seasoning in it. Cayenne pepper, salt, pepper, and hot sauce. If you are using frozen shrimp, make sure they are thawed out first. But fresh shrimp are much, much better. When the water comes to a boil, drop the shrimp in, and as soon as the water comes back to a boil, cut the heat off. Let them sit there for about five minutes and strain them. For the rémoulade sauce, use a mayonnaise jar, the quart size, and put mayonnaise in it until it's half full and add ketchup until it's three-fourths full. Then add yellow mustard and Worcestershire sauce. Shake all of that up, and you'll be surprised. Add it to the shrimp, and you are a chef.

The breakfasts I like are: liver and onions with grits and hot sausage and pancakes. For grits, I boil the water first and add melted margarine. Let it come back to a boil with salt and pepper. Then you pour the grits in. You have to keep stirring the grits, and you can't rush them or they will be lumpy. I use a long-handled wooden spoon. After they are done, put them aside. Then slice an onion very thin (don't dice it, slice it). Put margarine in the frying pan with the sliced onions and let them simmer down. Cut your liver very, very thin. The thinner it is, the better it will taste. Never let liver cook and then sit in its own gravy. I put the liver on the bottom of the pan and the onions on top and keep flipping it. After it begins to cook, you can put a cup of water over the liver and onion and stay there and watch it cook down. You don't really need to add flour that way because the liver will have its own lovely brown color. Put the liver and onions right over the grits.

For pancakes, I use my hands. I don't like an electric mixer. One cup of flour will make enough for three servings. One cup of flour, one egg. Six cups of flour, six eggs, and so on. Add a cup of milk and a dash of vanilla per cup of flour. Then I add just a pinch of baking powder. Very little so it won't rise up too high. Not more than half a teaspoon. Clean the grill thoroughly and put the margarine on it. Two flips, and you got it made.

Never put anything with dressing in it to warm up in an oven. Put it in a broiler. In an oven, it will come out flat. It will flatten right out.

Pickled pork is hard to get anywhere other than New Orleans. It's just fresh pork pickled the same way you do a cucumber. If you can't buy pickled pork tips, just get some fresh pork, cut it up, put it in a jar of vinegar, and let it soak for about two or three days. Then put it in the refrigerator. Pickled pork gives red beans a special taste. Soak the beans overnight with diced onion. But don't use the soaking water to cook them in. Drain if off because it's too salty. Put the beans in fresh water to cook. Sauté some onion, celery, and parsley with small, stew-size pieces of meat. Put it aside. In an hour and a half, the beans will start breaking up, and you'll begin to smell them. Wait another half-hour and then add the sautéed meat and the pickled-pork seasonings. The grease from the meat will line the pot. After two hours, you have to watch because the water will cook down, and you will have to add another three-fourths pot of water. Everybody knows that beans take from two to three hours, but you still have to watch it. When they start getting thick, you judge whether you want it thinner or not.

For the rice, start off with boiling water with a cup of vinegar in it and salt and pepper. Then put the rice in the boiling water.

We stir it to make sure it doesn't stick, and in no less than thirty minutes, it's ready. Strain it. If you are going to refrigerate the rice, take as much of the starch out as possible. You do that by pouring cold water over it at the sink. If you leave the starch in it, it will sour. If you want to keep the rice hot, put it in a strainer and place the strainer over a saucepan that has just enough water in it so it doesn't touch the strainer. Cover the rice and put it over a flame. It will steam and keep hot.

CHARLES BAILEY

Charles Bailey was fifteen years old when he started work at a career that has led him to the position of executive chef at the Grand Hotel. Twenty-seven years ago, he was a passeur and coffee maker at the old Jung Hotel. He was encouraged by the head chef there, Daniel Serpe, to study cooking. When he was in high school, Mr. Bailey wanted to be a great athlete and carried a gym bag around all the time, in spite of the fact that the coaches said he would never make it. But tucked down inside his gym bag with his shoes, shirts, and sports paraphernalia were his spatula and his knives. Here he talks about some of his favorite recipes.

Ninety percent of what I eat is fruit and seafood, and Lobster Armorican is one of my favorite dishes. The important thing in this recipe is the use of a Maine lobster. You can use a Florida lobster also, but a true Lobster Armorican uses a live Maine lobster. Split it in half while it is alive and separate the claws from the body. Then place it in the pan with the butter mixed with oil until it turns red. In the fat from a Maine lobster, you will find green particles. They look like poison, but they're the most delicate part of the lobster and really nutritious and better-tasting than the meat to a certain extent because that is where the flavor is coming from. So use them with the lobster. And don't let the lobster sit there after it's cooked. Once it is seared and turned red, take it out of the *sautoir*. Then add the bay leaves and vegetables. Make sure you don't peel any of them—not the tomato, carrots, or celery ribs—none of them. For the best taste, don't use water for the sauce, but use lobster stock or the stock from shellfish—shrimp, crawfish, any of them, but never a fish stock. Fish stock has a taste very different from a shellfish stock. The other important ingredient is the brandy ignited in the sauce. After this is stirred, strain it to get the bay leaf out and any lumps or particles that may have accumulated in the cooking. Then put the lobster back into the *sautoir* full of sauce and ignite it with a second dose of brandy. If you don't have a pinch of tarragon leaves, use a tiny dash of tarragon vinegar. Not much because you don't want to take away the aroma of the lobster or kill the flavor of the brandy. It will blend well, and actually the acid from the vinegar will bring out all the true flavors. The tomato paste is for color and taste, but you can use fresh tomatoes instead of the paste if you wish. But not tomato purée. When the sauce is done, you should be ready to serve because this is not a dish that can or should sit on a stove and simmer.

Another favorite of mine is Coq au Vin. This is a special, young rooster. It's cooked pretty much the same way people used to cook stewing hens, but this young rooster has tender flesh and firmer muscles. It should be precooked or presteamed. Put it in a pan with about two cups of water and cover it with aluminum foil. Stick it in the oven and cook it just enough to break the muscles and loosen them up—don't cook it completely. Then take it out and cut it in half. The breasts of this fowl are large, as large as a man's four fingers. Sauté the chicken breasts until they get a nice brown color. No flour need be used. Now my way is to make the sauce with oil and butter. The butter blends well with the heavy cream and brings out the color, too. When you make the sauce, remember that you can never make too much. That is, if you end up with more than you need for the dish, save it and add it to other things. Hamburger even. Anything that can use a meat sauce. There's never any waste with a sauce. You add a little wine, here red wine, a Burgundy, to perk up the sauce and enhance the color. In this recipe, I recommend using old-fashioned thick bacon, not the commercial bacon bits or the thin-sliced modern bacon. We used to use "streak of lean," the real thick pork. Dice it up into cubes and sauté it with the mushrooms, onions, and so on. Make sure the onions are white or yellow onions. The red onions have too much strength for this dish. If the red wine doesn't give you the nice color you want, you can add a mere drop of red food coloring.

The Scampi Conti is another favorite. Use the 10-to-15 count shrimp. They are a better grade, and you need a little tougher shrimp than for other dishes. After dipping the shrimp in the egg wash, barely dust them with flour. Don't saturate them in flour or leave the shrimp in flour so long that a crust is formed. Just dust them. But the real secret is to make sure you don't let the shrimp brown in the pan. Place the flour-dusted shrimp in the pan and cook them about five minutes. After you have mixed the shrimp with the sautéed seasonings, you add the pineapple. I use raisins in the rice; it makes the rice colorful, and with the pineapple in the shrimp, you get the sweetness separated. Don't cook the raisins, though. Just add them to the cooked rice and make it into a ring or mold to surround the shrimp and pineapple.

In the veal dishes, if the veal is milk-fed (that is, baby calf, not baby cow), don't use a tenderizer. Just pound it gently. It's very easy to tear, so be careful. Dust it with flour (no egg wash) and sauté it very, very lightly. It's a quick, delicate item.

The Roast Long Island Duckling is another special dish I like. The entire meat of a duckling, unlike that of a chicken, is one hundred percent dark meat. Most people overcook duckling. It's a very fragile and tasty fowl and should not be cooked that way. My procedure is to take a three- to four-pound duckling, and after salting and peppering it in preparation for roasting, stick a Washington Delicious apple, a paw of garlic, a rib of celery, a pinch of thyme, two bay leaves, and a pinch of rosemary inside the duckling. If you put seasonings and vegetables on the outside of the duckling in the pan, the fat will wash them away completely, but the heat inside the bird allows the flavor to expand throughout the duckling. Cook it from one and a half to two hours. In that time, it will be eighty-five to ninety percent cooked. You remove it from the oven and let it sit in its juices while you make the sauce. Let it cool completely. Use the drippings and flour for the roux. The roux should not be overly brown because we add a lot of sugar and half a pint of vinegar. Let the sugar and vinegar reduce until it is a caramel color, then pour it into the roux, and you will get a nice golden-brown color. You can also use half a pint of orange juice. After the sauce has reduced and you are ready to serve it, split the duckling in half and pour sherry over it and let it reduce. Don't leave it in too long, or the sherry will get thin and the duck will begin to fry in it. Then remove the duckling halves to a serving dish and pour the strained sauce over them.

A great dressing that can be easily prepared at home is the Lummie Salad Dressing. You can do it with a regular mixer, shaker, or blender. Break one egg into a mixing bowl with one cup olive or cooking oil and the red vinegar and seasonings. The oil has a tendency to thicken the egg, and the vinegar will dilute the thickness, so the blending is extremely important. The cheese must be a blue cheese and the mustard dry. Whip all the ingredients together in a blender at low speed for ten to fifteen minutes. You will be surprised how much sauce this one egg can create. One other thing: Since the egg will separate from the oil if the oil gets cold, don't put it in the refrigerator. Now you can add one tablespoon of cornstarch to hold it together better. But even if you see it separate and begin to look like clabbered milk, you don't have to discard it. Just take another whole egg and go through the whole process again—without adding more seasonings. You'll have the same results again and with a better body. The longer you whip it, the better it is.

I like pineapple juice in potato pancakes. Even though they already have onions in them (mostly for flavor but also to keep the potatoes from turning black), the pineapple juice gives a nice taste to the pancake.

HENRY CARR

Henry Carr has supervised as many as ninety-six people in his kitchens while he himself worked an average of fourteen hours a day, six days a week. He began cooking at La Louisiane on Iberville Street—first washing dishes, later as a cook's aid. After throwing some hash-browned potatoes over his arm while trying to flip them, the head cook, a Mr. Jeff Harris, took him aside and began to teach him the fundamentals. He mastered the skills and went from La Louisiane to the Court of Two Sisters, then to Brennan's, and later to Pascal's Manale, where he cooked and supervised for over seventeen years. His reputation and his expertise with food has benefited many famous restaurants in New Orleans.

Two of my favorites are Baked Lasagna and Creole Gumbo. The important thing about lasagna is putting it together. After you put the lasagna in the pan along with the meat sauce, you make it like a cake in the pan. Mix the ricotta cheese with the egg to loosen the cheese up. That's one layer. Then it's a masterful thing to watch the diced mozzarella cheese going into different places in the lasagna and the slices of egg with the white ring around the yellow yolk lying on top. Put a little parsley on to garnish it. It's beautiful, a sight to behold.

The gumbo requires some hard cooking—real Southern-style cooking. You use peeled shrimp, saving the shells and heads. Boil two gallons of stock and keep it boiling while you get the rest of the ingredients together. For the roux, use a cup of plain flour and cooking oil or olive oil. Make that into a paste—not runny but almost like a biscuit dough, although a little loose. Play with it until it gets good and hot and starts to cook. As it cooks you will see little flakes of brown at the bottom. Stir it and mix it up and let more flakes develop. Do that until it is golden brown. Then take a large white onion, three pieces of celery, one bell pepper, half a cup of the tips of the green onions, one #2 can of tomatoes, one pound shrimp, one and a half pounds of okra, four crabs (hard shell), four ounces dried shrimp, one-eighth ounce Tabasco sauce and about one and a half ounces of Worcestershire sauce, one teaspoon gumbo filé, and, of course, salt and pepper to taste. You need two gallons of shrimp stock and one pound of lump crabmeat. The crabmeat should be the last ingredient to go in—you don't want it to break up on you. Don't put it in until about three minutes before you stop cooking. The shrimp shells that you saved are boiled for your shrimp stock. Cook the okra dry and keep the stock boiling.

When I make mushroom canapés, I use breadcrumbs made from French bread. Wet. And you have to know how wet is wet. They shouldn't be soggy. Soak the bread, then drain it by putting it in a sieve and let it drip dry. Then break the bread up. When it's cooked, the wetness will leave, and the bread will tighten up. You know you can freeze French bread to keep it fresh. After five minutes in the oven, it's just like when they delivered it.

I don't like intensive heat on anything unless I'm sautéing. Then I'll use a very heavy pan. Don't put anything else in the pan you use to sauté. Cover it, put it on the burner, and keep it covered. When you're ready to sauté, drop in the ingredients. You'll hear it hiss like a steam engine. Raise the cover every now and then. That's when you want a fast seal—to seal the juices inside. Then you simmer it down with the sauces. When it's simmered all the way, you take it completely off the heat. It can sit for three or four hours that way with the cover on it. This is a good way to sauté chicken breasts when you want to retain the juices inside. After you've finished simmering, remove the pan from the flame and let it sit until the chicken's as tender as butter. If you're having a dinner party, do it in the afternoon and let it sit there and materialize for you.

I try never to use water for cooking. I prefer stock. I make it two or three days ahead and cook it just about that long. You have to keep straining it until it purifies—I have a strainer in my stockpots. Keep one stock for seafood, one for beef, one for chicken. Sometimes beef stock is good with some chicken stock added—it makes a good gravy. And the gelatin from a turkey should be saved. It makes a zesty stock, and you can't buy that taste in a store. Turkey gelatin is also good for basting broiled chicken. It shines when you baste it with gelatin. You get the gelatin after the fowl sits in the refrigerator a day or two. The juices turn to jelly.

The value of a pot is in its bottom. So I put my seasonings in all at once: thyme, oregano—they all get sautéed right along with the green seasonings. But you have to be careful about the amounts because spices can take the flavor away from a dish. Like sage. I use sage in a marinara sauce and a pan roast but very, very sparingly. And it's one seasoning where, if you use too much, you can't straighten it out later, and the dish is ruined. With spices you should go right to the brim—not over. The important thing is to enhance the taste of the food, not to drown it.

CORINNE DUNBAR'S

Corinne Dunbar's is a legendary New Orleans restaurant. The late Leona Victor and Clara Mathus were the original cooks at this restaurant, and Mrs. Victor trained Mrs. Mathus as well as Thelma Elsey, who is now semi-retired. Mrs. Victor was Mrs. Corinne Dunbar's personal cook, and the two of them began the restaurant in 1935 during the Depression. At present, the day staff consists of Virginia Griffin, Johnnie Mae Rodriguez, Albert Cantey, Irene Williams, Ruby Jefferson, Carrie Taylor, Eunice Harris, and Rosa Barganier. "Corinne Dunbar's is a family affair," says Mr. James Plauché, the owner—there are no chefs, no menu. Just one superb meal prepared by women who learned their art both from each other and from each generation of cooks that preceded them. The group works so well together that the owner says he can leave for three months at a time without worry. Here Rosa Barganier talks about cooking. She started at Dunbar's in 1960 washing dishes. She moved soon thereafter from kitchen help to second cook (vegetables) and became head cook when Clara Mathus died.

I've worked in hospitals, schools, clubs—all sorts of things, but this is what I enjoy. Sometimes it would give me a run for my money—mastering the duck, the dove, the squab—they almost mastered *me*. We prefry our Cornish hens. Put them in a deep fryer, let them brown, then put them in the oven with the sauce for about twenty minutes. We add pâté to our chicken stock and baste the hens with it. It makes a lovely gravy. In our stock, we use the juice of onions that we have diced for other dishes, and we sometimes boil thyme, bay leaf, or garlic and use the juice from that. This way we get the flavor of the seasoning without the pieces of seasoning in it. You should strain the stock as you use it, so there won't be any seasoning floating around. I use a blender a lot. I don't chop or dice onions myself. Grinding and blending is a lot of what I do to make sauces and gravies. Like the pecan sauce I make for chicken has a sausage patty in it, but it's blended so well you'd never notice it.

When we make red bean soup, we use fresh thyme and bay leaf, but I don't put them directly in the beans. I put them in a little bag and let it steep there, so when I strain the soup, I have gotten the taste of thyme and bay leaf, not the flakes. I grind the ham, onion, and celery and let it all cook together. A pinch of sugar takes the gas out of the beans.

In biscuits, you can't be too skimpy with the salt. After I mix the biscuit dough, I stick my finger in it to see if everything is just right. It has a certain feel when it's right. To keep them small—bite-size—I roll them very thin. Some biscuits are so large they intimidate you.

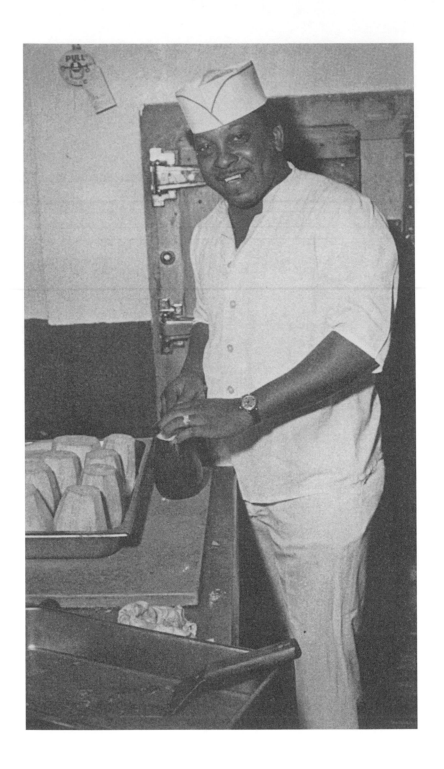

MALCOM ROSS

Malcom Ross began cooking while in the armed services, where he learned "the basic things": meats, soups, preparing a complete meal. After his tour in the Army, he managed a chicken franchise in New Orleans. For the last seven years, he has been a chef at the world-famous Galatoire's.

Everything I've learned about cooking French and Creole foods I learned at Galatoire's. I started there at the fry station under the direction of Willie Morrison. Then I moved to the broiler station and worked under Wallace Shelby. At the sauté station, I was taught by Warren Martin and Charlie Marshall. I have to give them all credit because I learned a lot from them. At the fry station, I had to do trout amandine, eggplant, shrimp, oysters brochette, onion rings—all the things Galatoire's is famous for. I also learned to make meunière sauce, which is a specialty of the house. At the broiler station, things are more difficult than at the fry station. We don't use timers or meat thermometers. You have to know when meat is rare, medium, medium-rare, or medium-well by sight and by feel. You have to learn all there is to know about broiling meat. How to cut the steaks (everything comes whole, and you have to butcher it), how to trim the fat, how to cut just about eight ounces of meat in such a way that you don't lose all the meat's properties. Meat and fillets have an excessive amount of fat, and when you trim them, you have to get a certain number of steaks out of each strip whether it's a fillet strip or a sirloin strip. Out of a fillet strip, you should get at least six to seven steaks. Out of a sirloin, you should get from ten to twelve steaks. I must say I rarely ever had a steak returned.

The sauté station is the hardest of all. There you prepare all the soups: oyster soup, consommé, cauliflower, broccoli. And all from fresh ingredients. And you have to make all of the sauces: Marchand de Vin, hollandaise—all the sauces Galatoire's is famous for. Customers come to us from everywhere. One man came from Saudi Arabia. He couldn't speak any English, but he had written on a piece of paper what he wanted: Trout Marguery. Within two years, I could cook everything on the menu. Anything that comes from the kitchen, I know how to make it.

The cream sauce is important when you make stuffed eggplant. You have to heat the milk separately and add the hot butter and flour roux to it. And the pots you cook it in should be very thick so it doesn't cook too fast. You blend it but not long enough to brown it. You add green onions (or chives—whichever you prefer), shrimp, salt, and pepper to the cooked meat of the eggplant. Roll it up like a football and place the mixture in the eggplant shells. Sprinkle with breadcrumbs and dot with butter and return to the oven or put in a warmer. That's it.

For the Trout Marguery, the hollandaise sauce is vital. I use pure butter, never margarine. It's a difficult sauce because you have to beat the yolks and add the butter at the same time, all the while cooking over water. You whip it with a whisk until the butter melts into the yolks. You let the eggs cook until they are almost scrambled. Then put the pan on the side away from the heat and add cold water, then whip it some more while it is off the flame. While you are whipping and adding butter, you put a little vinegar in to smooth it out. It takes two hands, but you have to do it the exact way—there are no short cuts. It will keep overnight at room temperature. Don't refrigerate it. The trout is rolled up and put in a pan with a little water and vinegar to keep it from sticking. Just enough water to cover the top of the fish so it won't burn. Put it in the oven for about fifteen minutes. Then you take a sauce made of shrimp and fresh mushrooms, a cream sauce, and a hollandaise. You mix all of these sauces together, heat them up (Marguery sauce can't be too hot), and after placing the trout in the center of the serving dish, pour the combined sauces over it. No garnish. Never use garnish with Trout Marguery. It's a fantastic dish.

LARRY WILLIAMSON

Larry Williamson is among the youngest of the New Orleans chefs. He began his career at Arnaud's and is now one of the excellent chefs at Galatoire's.

I don't season the fish when I fry it; I season the flour. When it is dipped in seasoned flour and fried in a deep fryer, it seems to hold its flavor better. I do the same with eggplant—season the flour, not the eggplant. Once in a while you can get an eggplant that is bitter—if you peel it and soak it in a little water, just enough to cover it, for over an hour, this will take some of the bitterness out. Then I batter the eggplant the same way I do the fish and deep-fry it.

There are two easy ways to skin tomatoes: One is to slip the tomatoes into warm water; the other is to put them in the basket of the deep-fry pot and move them around in the hot oil for about two minutes. The skin will pop off. Some cooks use only flour for their fried tomatoes; I use corn flour and breadcrumbs, and that gives them a nice taste. I probably use more eggs in my batter than other cooks do.

A lot of people overcook the butter in the meunière sauce. It should be a light brown—not dark brown. And I use the juice of fresh lemons and lemon concentrate in my meunière sauce, along with wine vinegar—it has to be wine vinegar.

When making Oysters Brochette, it's not a good idea to cook them ahead of time and warm them up before serving. Too much oil stays in them that way. They only take two or three minutes to fry, so you should wait until you are ready to serve them before you cook them. I prefer vegetable oil to peanut oil or even the oil we use in the restaurant because it holds the taste better.

If you are cooking a steak medium—don't put it completely under the broiler. It can cook too fast that way and lose some of its taste. Pull it back a little from the flame.

You have to experiment with the foods to get them right. And every cook has his own methods. I remember one chef, Wallace Shelby; he sautéed with the least amount of butter I've ever seen anybody use, and his things tasted better that way. He took much longer than most of us to make his sauces because he felt that the slower they cooked, the better they tasted. I think the whole secret of sauces is in the slow cooking: Creole sauce needs about an hour and a half, meunière sauce ten minutes, and Marchand de Vin about one hour over a slow fire.

In making stuffed eggplant, remember to put the seasoning in the flour, not on the eggplant. It will hold the flavor better. And some people don't warm the stuffing before they return it to the shell for browning, so sometimes it will be brown on the top and cold inside. You should take the stuffing and reheat it in a skillet for about two or three minutes before putting it in the eggplant shell and browning.

SHERMAN CRAYTON

Sherman Crayton began cooking at Arnaud's Restaurant in 1936.
His first jobs were in the kitchen: dishwasher, pot washer, and pas-
seur. On Carnival Day in 1938, he was given a job in the pantry.
Because he wanted to get further along than pantry cooking, he
started "going down the line" and watching the cooks. In 1939, he
started cooking with them, and by 1940 he held the dinner station
all by himself. After a tour of duty in the service, where he earned
the rating of Cook First Class, he returned to Arnaud's. Later he
worked at the Court of Two Sisters and in 1963 was offered the
position of chef at the Vieux Carré Restaurant.

You have to respect food. I don't even allow long fingernails in my
kitchen—they are a hazard to the food. Finesse is important in the
preparation of food, especially Creole food, which is special. They
say it is a mixture of Spanish and French, but the only people who
seem to know all about it are neither Spanish nor French, they're
Blacks. They got it from their grandparents and gave it its individual touch. Sautéing is a very important part of New Orleans
cooking—very little broiling—and so is the use of stocks.

Oysters Vieux Carré are a favorite of mine. Actually they're
an Oyster Suzette and easy to make. Dice the bacon and sauté
it. Leave the bacon in its own grease, but don't let it burn or get
hard. Add bell pepper chopped very fine and chopped pimento.
Add butter—not margarine because margarine in this recipe will
turn out to be nothing but grease with no flavor after it melts.
Butter is stronger. Then add a little Tabasco. Cook the oysters
right in their open shells, for a short time, just until the fringe
of the oyster curls. Drain the water off the oysters and pour the
sautéed mixture over them, then reheat.

Bouillabaisse is another favorite. For six people, you should
use three medium-size bell peppers, three medium white onions,

one half stalk of celery. Cut all this into large pieces. (When I say large, I don't mean cut it in half—I mean chop it up into bite-size pieces. But we don't want the pieces uniform in size.) Add two cloves of garlic, a bunch of green onions, and sauté all of these ingredients in one half cup of cooking oil. Add two cans of tomatoes and the same amount of water as one tomato can will hold. One lemon cut in half and then the fish. Put as many kinds of fish as you want in there. Redfish, red snapper, shrimp, oysters, crabmeat. Add a pinch of saffron and, after all of this is cooked, add a cup of white wine and salt and pepper to taste. It's a thin soup that will take any amount and variety of seafood, but you don't serve it with rice.

If you don't have beef stock, you can use beef consommé, but it's best to keep beef stock on hand. To make it, you boil beef bones, celery, and onion for about two hours. It will keep in the refrigerator for about two days—after that it will sour. But in the freezer it will stay fresh for a long, long time.

Shrimp Creole is one of the few Creole dishes that has no wine in it. One pound of peeled and deveined fresh shrimp sautéed in a stick of butter for ten minutes. Add three bell peppers and three medium white onions and a rib of celery. Make sure the onions and celery are chopped fine because they both take longer to cook than the peppers. Cook for ten more minutes. Add a can of crushed tomatoes, salt, pepper, two whole bay leaves, a little fresh thyme, and two cloves of garlic. Put the garlic in after the tomatoes because garlic burns very easily.

LOUISE JOSHUA AND LETITIA PARKER

Louise Joshua and Letitia Parker are two of the principal cooks at the famous Bon Ton Café. Mr. Al Pierce, the owner, started the restaurant in 1953. Originally it was located at 322 Magazine Street; they have been in their new location at 401 Magazine Street for seven years. Mr. Pierce's late wife did the cooking and training of all the people who worked in their restaurant. Mrs. Joshua has been cooking in the Pierce establishment for over thirty years. Mr. Pierce describes the cooking as more Cajun than Creole, and while he does not claim that his restaurant is better than any other, he admits he has never found one that was superior. Mr. Pierce generally speaks for his cooks, but they sometimes speak for themselves, as Mrs. Joshua and Mrs. Parker do below.

MRS. JOSHUA: When I make gumbo, I add the roux after the meats have cooked. That way the meat is tender, and it doesn't take so long to cook later on, when you are simmering the gumbo. And I don't pour the fats off the sausage and ham: It's nice to keep it in for flavoring. Also I don't put my roux into the gumbo until after the gumbo boils. Roux won't lump if you add it to boiling liquid. My mother never boiled her rice. She steamed it, and I do it the way she did. I wash the rice and measure it and the water, add salt, and let it boil covered until the water boils out. Then I lower the flame and let it steam. I check on it constantly and stir it around to feel the grains, then let it steam some more until the grains are free of each other.

MRS. PARKER: Olive oil is better for crabmeat dishes. In Crabmeat Imperial, for instance, it holds the crabmeat together better than butter, although it's all right to sauté the seasonings in butter.

ROCHESTER ANDERSON

Rochester Anderson was born in Jackson, Mississippi and started cooking at Baptist Hospital when he was eighteen years old. He had cooked a little at home in Mississippi but had no formal training. The chef at the hospital noticed how little he knew and began to teach him. His special interest in the cooking of game, acquired when he lived at home with his mother in Mississippi, has led him to achieve extraordinary skill in preparing venison, quail, and other game.

Cooking game birds takes a lot of time. You have to keep basting them even after they have begun to cook in the wine and seasonings. You have to pay close attention to them; you can't leave them alone the way you might with fowl or meat that isn't wild. Some people prefer white wine for basting, but my preference is a Burgundy. And it's important to remember that when cooking game, always use the very best wine. Cooking wine from the shelf of a grocery store won't do.

A seafood eater can easily tell the difference between a fish dish in a restaurant that has been thawed and one that contains fresh fish. The meat of thawed fish is tight; fresh fish is firm but soft. My favorites are trout and redfish—I like redfish better than trout. Trout is soft, and I prefer the coarseness of redfish and its sweeter taste.

When you prepare flounder, you cut off the fins and debone it. There are two or three ways of filleting a flounder. Some cooks simply split it open and take the whole bone out. My way is to split it halfway, leaving something like a pocket in there, and break the flounder. Pull half the bone out. That way you will leave two little pieces of bone in it: one at the front and one at the back. It will hold the fish together so that it keeps its shape after it has been stuffed. If you split it wide open, the stuffing, which is not firm when hot, may run out. And since I don't put any breadcrumbs in the stuffing, the deboning process is important. I don't like stuffing that is too tightly packed. And you should start your fish off in the oven and then put it in a broiler to brown. The oven is necessary to make sure it is cooked through. Broilers are fast and can leave food partially cooked. Especially when cooking at home, use the oven.

Here in New Orleans, we save oil and drippings from cooking meat and use it again. You have to strain it each time and remember not to use fish oil for anything other than fish and chicken drippings for very different meat. An easy way to strain oil is to take a piece of plain Idaho potato, cut it up, and let it cook right in the oil you have just used. Leave the potato in it overnight, and it will clear the oil right up. If you take the trimmings from the meat you are cooking and reduce them to oil, it can be used for deep-frying. It adds a wonderful flavor.

CHARLES KIRKLAND

Charles Kirkland began his career in the New Orleans food business in 1932, when he took a job as a bus boy in the cafeteria of the LaSalle Hotel. Later that year, he worked as a passeur at the Touro Infirmary. By 1935, he was cooking at the Court of Two Sisters, where he earned thirty-eight cents an hour. In spite of the discouraging wages, he and his fellow workers were delighted with the owner's policy of letting them work "as long as they wanted to." Mr. Kirkland remembers working seventeen hours a day for most of the seven years he stayed there. In 1942, he began to work at Commander's Palace, where he remained for twenty-seven years, handling the dressings and salads station by himself. It was not unusual for him to serve 700 customers a night, some 900 on weekends, and during an especially heavy evening, he served as many as 1,000. An undisputed specialist in salads and dressings of all kinds, Mr. Kirkland is now semiretired and working part-time at Broussard's, where he still makes some of the best dressings in town.

Never wait until a salad dressing is completed before you taste it. While you are preparing it, taste it as you go along. Some salad dressings should be made in small quantities, even if you are serving a lot of people. Oil-and-vinegar dressing, for example, should be prepared this way because constant use causes it to lose its flavor. Neither is it a good idea to be too thrifty with salad dressing. I mean, if you have a little left over from one dinner, you may want to add it to a fresh batch for another dinner. I don't recommend it. Make your dressing fresh each time.

Don't refrigerate a garlic dressing. Not only will it lose its flavor when chilled, other foods in the refrigerator will pick up the garlic odor. Room temperature brings out the flavor of a garlic dressing.

New potatoes don't make good potato salad. They tend to be hard at the center when cooked. The Idaho potato is always preferable. Boil it in its own jacket—don't peel it before you cook it—so that the flavor and nutrients will stay intact. The more eggs you add to a potato salad, the better it is. Skimping on the eggs makes a less tasty salad.

Be cautious with mayonnaise if you are mixing it with crabmeat. Unlike shrimp, the crabmeat can be easily overwhelmed by the flavors of ingredients added to it. Crabmeat has a very delicate taste, and the purpose of any ingredient added to it is not to overwhelm or bury that taste.

Pay very close attention to what you are doing when you make dressings and salads. Some people believe that salad is the easiest part of the meal to prepare, and they are very casual about it. The result may be a casual, dull-tasting salad. It requires your full attention in the preparation if you expect your guest's full attention to it at the table.

PART TWO:
RECIPES

APPETIZERS

Oysters en Brochette
LARRY WILLIAMSON

½ pound bacon
3 dozen oysters, drained
2 cups flour (enough to cover oysters thoroughly)
1 teaspoon salt
1 teaspoon pepper

Vegetable oil for frying (do not use peanut or soybean oil)

Egg Wash
3 eggs, beaten
1½ cups milk

Cut bacon strips in half and cook lightly. They should not be crisp. Alternating two oysters with two pieces of bacon, place on six skewers. Make sure oysters and bacon are very close together. Continue until skewers are full. Season the flour with salt and pepper. Combine eggs and milk in a shallow bowl. Dip skewers in egg wash, then in seasoned flour. Fry in a 3-quart deep fryer at 360° for 4 minutes. Remove skewers. *Serves 6*

Oysters Rockefeller I
AUSTIN LESLIE

½ pound butter (or margarine, if preferred)
3 pounds fresh spinach
4 stalks green onion
4 parsley sprigs and leaves
½ head iceberg lettuce
½ cup breadcrumbs
1 teaspoon green food coloring

½ cup Herbsainte liqueur (see Glossary, p. 317)
3 dozen oysters, boiled*
3 dozen clean oyster shells
½ cup grated parmesan cheese

Preheat broiler to medium heat. Melt butter and set aside. Grind spinach, onions, parsley, and lettuce in a food processor and place in a mixing bowl. Stir in breadcrumbs (reserving a small amount for later), the food coloring, and Herbsainte and place mixture in a blender. Purée at fast speed until creamy (about 2 minutes). Place the boiled oysters in the shells and cover with the puréed mixture. Sprinkle with cheese and reserved bread-crumbs. Place under the broiler for 20 minutes. Dot with a little melted butter before serving. *Serves* 6

* To cook oysters, bring them to a boil in their own liquid. As soon as boiling point is reached, remove from heat. Let oysters sit in the hot liquid until you are ready to use them.

Oysters Rockefeller II
SHERMAN CRAYTON

1 stick of butter	Salt and pepper to taste
1½ cups flour	1 teaspoon Tabasco sauce
2 cups Beef Stock (p. 213) or beef consommé	3 tablespoons sherry
	¼ cup Herbsainte liqueur (see Glossary, p. 317)
2 pounds fresh spinach	
2 bunches parsley	18 oysters
3 bunches green onions (enough to make 2 ½ to 3 cups)	18 clean oyster shells

Preheat oven to 350°. Melt butter in a saucepan. Add flour to it and cook long enough to make a brown roux. Slowly stir in the beef stock. Remove stems from spinach and parsley. Wash vegetables and grind as fine as possible. Add vegetables to the roux-beef stock mixture and place in an uncovered Dutch oven over low heat for 1½ hours, stirring periodically to avoid sticking. Add salt, pepper, and Tabasco and blend to the consistency of a paste. Remove from heat and stir in sherry and Herbsainte. Pour into a separate pan to cool. Place the oysters on the half shells and put in oven for 5 minutes, just until the oysters have curled.

Remove oysters from shells, drain, return to shells, and top with cooled sauce. Return to oven and bake for 15 minutes. *Serves 3*

Oysters Bienville I
AUSTIN LESLIE

3 dozen oysters, boiled
3 dozen clean oyster shells
½ cup Bienville Sauce
 (p. 240), cold
½ cup breadcrumbs

½ cup grated parmesan
 cheese
1 ounce butter, melted (or
 margarine, if preferred)

Preheat broiler at high flame or oven to 350°. Place boiled oysters in shells and cover with cold Bienville sauce. Top with the breadcrumbs and cheese and place on cookie sheet. Pour melted butter over oysters to moisten and place under broiler for 4 to 5 minutes, or in a 350° oven for 7 to 10 minutes. *Serves 6*

Oysters Bienville II
SHERMAN CRAYTON

18 oysters on the half shell
1½ cups flour
1 stick butter (or margarine,
 if preferred)
2 cups fish stock (see below)
2 cups fresh shrimp, shelled,
 boiled, and finely chopped
1 medium-sized white onion,
 finely chopped
4 ribs celery, finely chopped
2 cups fresh mushrooms,
 finely chopped

1 cup milk
½ cup white wine
½ cup sherry
½ cup grated parmesan
 cheese

Fish Stock
½ pound fishbones
2 whole paws of garlic, peeled
2 bay leaves
½ gallon water

For fish stock, boil all ingredients for one hour. Strain. Preheat oven to 350°. To prepare oysters, follow procedure for Oysters Rockefeller II (p. 108). Make a white roux and add the strained fish stock. Add the shrimp, onions, celery, mushrooms, and milk to the stock-roux mixture. Simmer 1½ hours over low heat. Add the white wine and sherry. Pour into a separate pan and allow to cool. When cooled, pour mixture over prebaked oysters and sprinkle with cheese. Put on baking sheet and bake in oven for about 20 minutes. *Serves 3*

Oysters Vieux Carré
SHERMAN CRAYTON

6 strips bacon, cut in pieces
2 medium green bell peppers, finely chopped
½ cup pimentos, finely chopped

2 ounces butter (do not substitute margarine in this recipe)
1 tablespoon Tabasco sauce
18 oysters on the half shell

Preheat oven to 350°. Sauté bacon. Do not let it get hard or burn and do not remove the bacon from its grease. Add peppers, pimentos, butter, and Tabasco. Sauté lightly and set aside. Place oysters on clean half shells and bake on a baking sheet in oven until they begin to curl at the edges (approximately 5 minutes). Drain water from oysters and cover with sautéed mixture. Return to oven and bake for 15 minutes. *Serves 6 (3 oysters per serving)*

Note: Oysters Rockefeller, Bienville, and Vieux Carré may be cooked and served over a bed of rock salt placed in the bottom of a baking pan. Be sure to let sauce for all of these oyster dishes cool before topping oysters and returning to oven.

Oysters Burton
NATHANIEL BURTON

1 dozen raw oysters
1 bay leaf
Dash of Worcestershire sauce
4 slices bacon, uncooked

1 cup flour
Egg Wash (p. 107)
2 cups fine breadcrumbs
Oil for frying

Poach oysters in their juices with bay leaf and Worcestershire sauce. Cut bacon slices into thirds, wrap each oyster with bacon, and fasten with a toothpick. Roll in flour, dip in egg wash, then roll in breadcrumbs. Deep-fry at 325° about 5 minutes. *Serves* 4

Oysters Odette
LOUIS EVANS

1 heaping teaspoon butter
½ tablespoon lard
2 medium red onions
   (enough to make 1 cup),
   finely chopped
1 tablespoon parsley, finely
   chopped
Pinch of thyme
1 large rib celery, finely
   chopped
2 teaspoons dry mustard
1 teaspoon yellow prepared
   mustard

½ cup fresh mushrooms,
   finely chopped
1 slice bread, cut in pieces and
   soaked in oyster water
2 dozen large or 3 dozen small
   oysters, and an equal number of clean oyster shells
1 egg, beaten
Cracker crumbs
Butter
Lemon slices for garnish

Preheat oven to 350°. Melt the butter and lard in an iron skillet. Add onion, parsley, thyme, celery, two types of mustard, and mushrooms. Cook until the vegetables are tender. Add the soaked bread and the oysters. Blend mixture thoroughly and simmer over low heat for 3 to 5 minutes. Fold in beaten egg and remove from stove. Do not cook after the egg has been added. Pile mixture into oyster shells, sprinkle with cracker crumbs, and dot with butter. Heat thoroughly in oven. Serve garnished with lemon slices. *Serves 8 to 9 (3 to 4 oysters per person)*

Barbecued Shrimp
LARRY WILLIAMSON

½ pound butter
2 dozen fresh jumbo shrimp,
    shells intact
6 tablespoons pepper*

½ cup Worcestershire sauce
2 teaspoons salt
2/3 cup ketchup

Melt butter in a saucepan over medium flame. Add shrimp and cook for 5 minutes. Add remaining ingredients and cook for 7 more minutes over a very low flame. *Serves 4*

* Or less if a milder sauce is preferred.

Les Huîtres Maison
SHERMAN CRAYTON

18 oysters, drained
½ cup flour
1 stick butter

3 garlic cloves, minced
2 tablespoons parsley,
    chopped

Dip oysters lightly in flour. Sauté in butter for 3 to 5 minutes. Sprinkle garlic and parsley over oysters. *Serves 6*

Crabmeat Remick

LOUIS EVANS

1 pound fresh lump crabmeat, drained

2 cups Mayonnaise (p. 244, or use ready-made)

1 teaspoon celery salt

1 teaspoon dry mustard

½ cup chili sauce (see Glossary, p. 315)

2 tablespoons paprika

1 ounce tarragon vinegar

3 strips bacon, cooked and broken in half

Preheat oven to 450°. Divide crabmeat into 6 portions on oven-proof plates or in ramekins. Blend mayonnaise, celery salt, mustard, chili sauce, paprika, and vinegar. Mix well. Place bacon on top of crabmeat and cover with mayonnaise mixture. Place ramekins in preheated oven for no more than 5 minutes (if broiler is used, 3 minutes). *Serves* 6

Crabmeat Louie

CHARLES BAILEY

1 rib celery

½ fresh pineapple, peeled and finely diced

8 ounces Grand Marnier

2 pounds choice fresh lump crabmeat

2 cups Mayonnaise (p. 244, or use ready-made)

1 cup ketchup

Salt

White pepper

Scrape celery and slice diagonally into paper-thin pieces. Put celery and pineapple in a bowl and cover with Grand Marnier. Let stand for 45 minutes to 1 hour. Strain juices from crabmeat and set aside. Place mayonnaise and ketchup in a bowl and mix well. Add crabmeat and mix gently. Try not to break the lumps of the crabmeat. Add salt and pepper to taste. Add celery-pineapple mixture. Toss and serve over a bed of lettuce. *Serves* 6 *to* 8

Crabmeat Dip
ROCHESTER ANDERSON

1 clove garlic, cut in half
1 8-ounce package cream
   cheese, at room temperature
1 pound fresh crabmeat
2 teaspoons lemon juice
1½ teaspoons Worcestershire
   sauce

Dash salt
Freshly ground pepper
1 small can chopped clams,
   drained

Rub a bowl with the cut garlic. Soften cream cheese over hot water in a double boiler. Transfer it to the bowl and add all remaining ingredients. Mix well and chill. Serve with unsalted crackers. *Makes 2 cups*

Crabmeat Biarritz
LOUIS EVANS

½ head of lettuce, either leafy,
   iceberg, or Boston
6 fresh artichokes, boiled
6 slices tomato
2 pounds fresh lump
   crabmeat
1 teaspoon parsley, chopped
1 rib celery, finely chopped

Salt and pepper to taste
1 cup Mayonnaise (p. 244, or
   use ready-made)
½ cup whipping cream,
   whipped for 5 minutes
1 teaspoon capers
1 teaspoon black caviar

Cover bottom of 6 plates with lettuce leaves. Place artichoke hearts in center of plate and cover each heart with a slice of tomato. Mix crabmeat with parsley, celery, salt, pepper, and ½ cup of the mayonnaise. Using a demitasse cup as a mold, place a small mound of the crabmeat mixture on top of each tomato. Arrange leaves from artichokes around each serving dish. Fold remainder of mayonnaise into the whipped cream. Blend thoroughly and place on top of each mound of crabmeat. Top with capers and caviar. *Serves 6*

Mushroom Canapés
HENRY CARR

½ pound clarified butter (see Glossary, p. 315)
½ cup green onions, chopped
1 cup freshly grated French breadcrumbs
4 ounces French bread moistened in water

1 ounce Worcestershire sauce
6 drops Tabasco sauce
Salt and pepper
1 pound fresh lump crabmeat
1 dozen large mushroom caps
1½ cups Hollandaise Sauce I (p. 238)

Preheat oven to 450°. Place clarified butter in saucepan over low flame. Add green onions and cook 1 minute. Stir in breadcrumbs and add the moist French bread. Add Worcestershire, Tabasco, and salt and pepper to taste. Fold in crabmeat. Cool. Roll into 12 2-ounce balls. Place on the mushroom caps. Bake in oven for 10 minutes. Top with hollandaise sauce. *Serves 6 (2 canapés per serving)*

Tomatoes Haley
CHARLES BAILEY

3 medium tomatoes
Salt
White pepper

Butter Sauce
1 stick of butter
2 to 3 cloves garlic, minced
1½ ounces freshly parsley, finely chopped

Preheat oven to 400°. Core tomato tops with paring knife and cut tomatoes in half. Salt and pepper them and set aside. Make Butter Sauce as follows: Whip butter with garlic and parsley until fluffy. Let stand at room temperature. When sauce is ready, place tomatoes in a baking pan or on a baking sheet. Reduce oven to 350° and bake tomatoes for 6 to 8 minutes. Remove from oven and place on a serving platter. Top with a generous serving of Butter Sauce. The heat of the tomatoes will melt the butter. *Serves* 6

Shrimp and Oysters Brochette
NATHANIEL BURTON

12 slices bacon
12 fresh mushroom caps, medium size
24 fresh jumbo shrimp, peeled and deveined
24 oysters

Cut each bacon slice into four pieces and sauté *very* lightly. Starting with the mushroom caps, alternately thread the bacon, shrimp, and oysters onto 2 8-inch skewers, ending with a mushroom on the tip of the skewer. Pan-broil for 6 minutes, remove from the skewers, and serve on toast. *Serves* 6

Escargots Bordelaise
MALCOM ROSS

12 dozen escargots
3 ounces butter, melted
1 whole paw of garlic, medium size, minced
½ cup fresh parsley, chopped

Put snails in pan with butter and heat just until hot. Stir in garlic. Put in individual serving dishes, sprinkle with parsley, and serve hot. *Serves* 12 (1 *dozen snails per serving*)

Cheese Straws

ANNIE LAURA SQUALLS

1 stick butter
2 cups sharp cheese, grated
1½ cups sifted flour

1 teaspoon baking powder
½ teaspoon salt
¼ teaspoon cayenne pepper

Preheat oven to 400°. Cream butter thoroughly. Add cheese and blend well. Stir in the dry ingredients. Roll out mixture to ½-inch thickness and cut into ½-inch wide strips. Place strips on greased baking sheet and bake in preheated oven 15 minutes, or until brown. *Makes* 4 *dozen*

SEAFOOD

Pompano en Papillote

LARRY WILLIAMSON

3 pompano tenderloins—
makes 6 fillets
½ pound small, fresh boiled
shrimp
2 dozen raw oysters
1 cup fresh mushrooms,
sliced
6 egg yolks, unbeaten
4 cups Cream Sauce II (p. 235)

¼ cup green onions, chopped
2 tablespoons fresh parsley,
finely chopped
¾ cup sherry
Salt
White pepper
6 papillote papers (see
Glossary, p. 317)
¼ cup cooking oil

Preheat oven to 350°. Place pompano in enough cold water to cover and boil rapidly for 5 minutes. Drain and set aside. In a deep (12-inch) pot, mix shrimp, oysters, mushrooms, egg yolks, cream sauce, green onions, parsley, and sherry. Add salt and pepper to taste. Place over low heat and simmer for 5 minutes. Remove from heat.

Lay out papillote papers and grease both sides with cooking oil. Spread ⅓ cup (about 6 tablespoons) of sauce mixture on each paper. Place pompano on top of sauce and pour another ⅓ cup of sauce on top of each pompano. Fold paper into bags and seal. Put bags on a baking sheet and heat in oven for 4 minutes. *Serves 6*

Fried Catfish I

NATHANIEL BURTON

¼ cup flour
1 cup corn meal
Salt
Pepper

Egg Wash (p. 107)
6 6-ounce catfish fillets
Oil for frying
Lemon wedges

Mix flour and corn meal thoroughly and season with salt and pepper. Dip fish in egg wash, then roll in flour and meal mixture. Deep-fry at 325° for 5 or 6 minutes. Place on platter and garnish with lemon wedges. *Serves* 4 *to* 6

Fried Catfish II
LEAH CHASE

2 catfish, weighing from 2 to
   3 pounds each
Salt
Pepper

1½ cups corn flour
   (see Glossary, p. 315)
2 cups peanut oil

Tenderloin the catfish (i.e., remove the skin and fillet them) and season with salt and pepper. Put corn flour in large brown paper bag. Shake catfish in corn flour until well covered. Heat oil in skillet and fry the catfish well on each side until golden brown. *Serves* 4

Trout Marguery I
AUSTIN LESLIE

3 2½-pound trout tenderloins
4 ounces margarine, melted
   (or butter, if preferred)
Salt and pepper to taste
3 cups Bienville Sauce (p. 240)
½ cup breadcrumbs

½ cup grated cheese, mild
   Cheddar suggested
1 lemon, thinly sliced
½ clove garlic, minced
6 sprigs parsley, finely
   chopped

Preheat broiler. Arrange trout in baking pan that has been greased with margarine. Brush fish with remaining margarine and season with salt and pepper. Place in broiler for 5 minutes. Remove from broiler and place on heatproof serving platter. Top with Bienville and sprinkle with breadcrumbs and cheese.

Return to broiler for 5 minutes. Garnish with sliced lemon, garlic, and parsley. *Serves 6*

Trout Marguery II
MALCOM ROSS

4 8 ounce trout tenderloins
2 tablespoons cooking oil or
  vinegar
½ pound fresh mushrooms,
  boiled, drained, and
  chopped
2 cups Cream Sauce II (p. 235)

2 cups Hollandaise Sauce II
  (p. 239)
1 pound cooked shrimp,
  peeled, deveined and
  chopped

Preheat oven to 350°. Roll up trout and place in a baking pan with enough water to cover the fish. Add cooking oil or vinegar to prevent fish from sticking to pan. Place in oven for 25 minutes. Combine mushrooms, cream sauce, hollandaise, and shrimp in saucepan. Heat slowly over a low flame for 3 minutes; avoid overheating. Place trout on platter and top with the sauce. Do not garnish. *Serves 4*

Trout Meunière
AUSTIN LESLIE

2 ½ cups peanut oil
3 2½-pound trout tenderloins
  (halved)
1 cup flour
½ cup margarine
½ cup white wine

1 lemon, sliced
½ clove garlic, finely chopped
6 sprigs parsley, finely
  chopped
Salt and pepper to taste

Preheat oil in frying pan to 350°. Test temperature by dropping a small amount of water in the oil to see if it pops. Dredge trout evenly in flour and fry, 2 pieces at a time, over medium flame for a total of 10 to 14 minutes, or 5 to 7 minutes on each side. After all 6 pieces are fried, place on a platter to keep warm. Heat the margarine with the wine and pour over the trout. Garnish with lemon slices, garlic, and parsley. Add salt and pepper to taste. *Serves 6*

Trout Véronique
LOUIS EVANS

2 6-ounce tenderloins of
    speckled trout
½ cup Sauterne
½ teaspoon salt

1 whole lemon
8 white grapes
1 cup Louis Evans's
    Hollandaise Sauce (p. 240)

Place trout in flat pan. Add wine and salt and squeeze juice from the whole lemon over it. Poach trout in the oven or atop stove over a low flame. If oven is used, preheat to 450° and bake 5 to 10 minutes. Transfer fish to a serving plate. Seed grapes, split in half, and place down the center of the fish. Pour hollandaise sauce over trout and brown under broiler for approximately 3 minutes. *Serves 2*

Stuffed Trout
LOUIS EVANS

6 8-ounce fillets of speckled
    trout
1 pound small fresh shrimp,
    peeled and deveined
4 cups water
¼ cup flour
½ pound butter
1 bunch green onions, chopped

½ cup sherry
Salt and pepper to taste
1 bay leaf
1 pound fresh lump crabmeat
½ cup Sauterne
2 cups milk
1 cup Louis Evans's
    Hollandaise Sauce (p. 240)

Preheat oven to 450°. Pound trout fillets well. Put shrimp in water and bring to a boil. Drain and set aside, reserving shrimp stock. In a small pan, combine 1 tablespoon of the flour, ¼ pound of the butter, and the green onions, and simmer 3 to 5 minutes over medium flame. Add shrimp stock, sherry, salt, pepper, and bay leaf and simmer until thick. Fold in crabmeat and shrimp and simmer for 5 to 10 minutes. Set aside to cool.

When cool, put a little of the mixture in each trout fillet. Roll the fillets and secure them with toothpicks. Arrange the fillets in a baking pan and pour the Sauterne over and around the fish. Cover with foil and poach in oven for 15 to 20 minutes. Remove pan from oven. In a saucepan, make a white roux of the remaining butter and flour and cook for 3 to 5 minutes. Add milk slowly and stir. Pour the wine sauce from the fish pan into the milk mixture and simmer over a low flame. Fold in hollandaise sauce. Remove fish and place on serving plate. Pour wine and hollandaise mixture over fish. *Serves* 6

Trout Eugène

LOUIS EVANS

1 7-8-ounce trout fillet	Juice of ½ lemon
¼ pound butter	1 teaspoon chopped parsley
1 green onion, finely chopped	2 ounces lump crabmeat
4 large shrimp, peeled and	
deveined	

Sauté trout in half the butter until golden. Set aside and keep warm. In another pan, melt remaining butter and add onion, shrimp, and lemon juice. Cook 5 to 6 minutes. Add parsley and crabmeat and toss with shrimp. Cover trout with shrimp and crabmeat mixture. *Serves* 1

Trout Amandine

NATHANIEL BURTON

½ pound almonds, blanched and split
1 pound butter
6 8-ounce trout fillets
Egg Wash (p. 107)

1½ cups seasoned flour (include 1 tablespoon salt and 1 tablespoon white pepper)
1 tablespoon fresh parsley, chopped
Juice of 2 lemons

Toast almonds in 4 ounces of the butter. Melt 4 additional ounces of butter in skillet. Dip trout in egg wash, then roll in seasoned flour. Place in skillet and brown on both sides until golden. Remove trout to platter. Brown remaining butter. Add parsley and lemon juice. Spoon butter over trout and top with the almonds. *Serves* 6

Trout Gresham

RAYMOND THOMAS, SR.

2 2-pound trout tenderloins
¼ pound butter
½ cup flour
1 cup milk

1 bunch green onions, finely chopped
1 clove garlic, minced
½ cup white wine
Salt and white pepper

Tenderloin the trout (i.e., fillet and remove the skin). Melt butter in a saucepan and add flour to make a roux. Stir for 5 minutes. Heat milk and add it slowly to the roux. Cook until thick. Add green onions, garlic, and wine and blend well. Cook sauce until smooth (approximately 5 minutes). Add salt and pepper to taste. Brush fish with a small amount of additional melted butter and broil until golden or bake in 350° oven for 7 minutes. Place fish on serving platter and cover with the sauce. *Serves* 4

Stuffed Flounder I

NATHANIEL BURTON

6 flounder, each weighing
  about 1 pound
1 green bell pepper, seeded
  and finely chopped
1 white onion, finely chopped
2 ribs celery, finely chopped
1 stick butter

½ loaf stale French bread
2 cups milk
1 pound fresh crabmeat
Salt and pepper to taste
¼ cup parmesan cheese,
  grated

Preheat oven to 375°. Debone flounder and place on baking sheet. To make stuffing: Sauté vegetables in butter until tender. Soak bread in milk and squeeze dry. Add bread and crabmeat to vegetables and mix thoroughly. Season with salt and pepper. Top flounder with the mixture and sprinkle with parmesan cheese. Bake at 375° for 25 minutes. *Serves* 6

Stuffed Flounder II

RAYMOND THOMAS, SR.

½ loaf stale French bread
2 green bell peppers, seeded
  and finely chopped
2 ribs celery, finely chopped
2 cloves garlic, minced

1 pound frozen crabmeat,
  thawed
2 sticks butter, melted
6 12-ounce flounder (bone
  removed)

Preheat broiler to 350°. Soak bread in water until soft and drain well. Sauté bread, vegetables, garlic, and crabmeat in melted butter until cooked, approximately 12 minutes. Insert mixture in flounder. Put under broiler for 5 minutes. Top with pan drippings. *Serves* 6

Redfish Court Bouillon I

RAYMOND THOMAS, SR.

3 pounds redfish, whole, with heads intact (8 ounces each)
½ cup cooking oil
1 white onion, chopped
½ rib celery, chopped
½ green bell pepper, chopped
½ bunch green onions (about ½ cup), chopped

1 clove garlic, minced
1 quart Fish Stock (p. 214)
1 8-ounce can whole tomatoes
1 8-ounce can tomato sauce
1 bay leaf, fresh
1 sprig of thyme

Preheat oven to 350°. Fillet the redfish, saving heads and spine, and set aside. To make stock, bring heads and spine to a boil in 1 quart of water and simmer for 20 minutes. Strain and cool to room temperature. Cut redfish fillets into hand-size portions. Place in baking pan and sprinkle with cooking oil. Bake about 10 minutes, or until done. Set aside and keep warm. Sauté vegetables and garlic in additional cooking oil until tender. Add tomatoes, tomato sauce, bay leaf, and thyme to the stock and cook over low flame for 30 minutes more. Pour sauce over fish and return to oven for 10 minutes. *Serves 4 to 6*

Redfish Court Bouillon II

MALCOM ROSS

4 4-ounce pieces of redfish (about 5 inches long)
½ cup flour
4 cups cooking oil
4 cups Creole Sauce (p. 238)

Dredge fish in flour and deep-fry in oil for 5 minutes at 360°. Heat Creole sauce in a pan and let simmer over a low flame for approximately 5 minutes. Put cooked fish in the sauce and let simmer for 10 minutes. Serve with rice or top rice with Creole sauce. *Serves* 4

Redfish Fillets My Way

LEAH CHASE

6 6-ounce redfish fillets	6 large lettuce leaves
1 pound fresh crabmeat	2 tablespoons flour
½ pound butter	1½ cups heavy cream
½ cup shallots, chopped	1 egg, beaten
1 teaspoon parsley, chopped	Salt and white pepper to taste
1 clove garlic, chopped	1 tablespoon Worcestershire
¼ teaspoon paprika	sauce
⅛ teaspoon cayenne	4 ounces Sauterne
½ cup breadcrumbs	

Preheat oven to 350°. Place fillets, skin side down, in a greased baking pan and set aside. Pick over crabmeat thoroughly. Melt 1 tablespoon of the butter in a saucepan, add the shallots, half of the crabmeat, the parsley, garlic, paprika, and cayenne. Cook until the shallots are translucent. Add breadcrumbs, remove from heat, and let cool. Spoon crabmeat mixture on fillets. Wilt the lettuce by pouring boiling water over the leaves. Roll the fillets and wrap in lettuce leaves. Return to baking pan. Cover tightly and bake for 45 minutes.

Melt remaining butter in pot. Add flour to make a roux. Stir while cooking 3 to 5 minutes. Gradually add cream, slowly stirring to keep mixture smooth. Add egg, white pepper, and salt to taste, stirring constantly. Add remaining crabmeat, Worcestershire sauce, and wine and cook 3 minutes. Remove from heat. Take stuffed rolls of fish from oven and place on serving platter. Pour crabmeat sauce over the fish. *Serves* 6

Redfish Thomas
RAYMOND THOMAS, SR.

2 pounds redfish fillets (8 ounces each)
Salt and pepper
1 stick butter, melted

1 small can crabmeat or 6 ounces frozen crabmeat (thawed)
Juice of 2 lemons
Chopped fresh parsley

Cut fish into hand-size portions and sprinkle with salt and pepper. Brush fish with a little of the melted butter and pan fry for 10 minutes. Sauté crabmeat in pan with remaining butter. Add lemon juice. Top fish with crabmeat and lemon-butter sauce from pan. Sprinkle with parsley. *Serves* 4

Stuffed Redfish
SHERMAN CRAYTON

6 7-ounce pieces of redfish tenderloin
1 recipe stuffing for Crêpes Maritimes (p. 270)

Preheat oven to 300°. Cut a pocket or pouch in the flank of each tenderloin. Add stuffing. Bake in an ungreased baking pan for approximately 20 minutes, or until fish is tender. *Serves* 6

Redfish with Tomato Sauce
NATHANIEL BURTON

¼ cup vegetable shortening
1 green bell pepper, seeded and finely chopped
1 medium white onion, finely chopped
1 #2½ can tomatoes, crushed
1 bay leaf (fresh, if possible)
1 sprig of thyme
2 tablespoons fresh parsley, chopped
Salt and pepper to taste
6 8-ounce redfish steaks
1 lemon

Preheat oven to 400°. Make tomato sauce: Melt shortening in a pan, add green pepper and onion, and cook until tender. Add tomatoes, bay leaf, thyme, 1 tablespoon of the parsley, salt, and pepper. Let cook at least 20 minutes. Put redfish in baking pan. Slice lemon thinly and place 1 slice on each fish steak. Bake in oven for 10 minutes. Pour sauce over fish, reduce oven to 350°, and bake 20 minutes more. Sprinkle with remaining parsley. *Serves 6*

Chef Louis Red Snapper with Crawfish Sauce
LOUIS EVANS

1 pound crawfish tails, peeled
1 quart water
1 bay leaf
Dash ground thyme
Salt and pepper to taste
1 teaspoon chicken base (or 1 chicken bouillon cube)
2 sticks butter
2 tablespoons flour
½ bunch green onions, chopped
2 ounces Sauterne
6 7-ounce red snappers
Melted butter

Preheat oven to 400°. Place crawfish tails in water and bring to a boil. Add bay leaf, thyme, salt, pepper, and chicken base. Remove from heat. In another pot, melt the butter and stir in the flour to make a rich roux. Simmer for 3 to 4 minutes. Add crawfish broth and tails and green onions to the roux and simmer for an additional 10 minutes. Add wine and let cook for 10 minutes more over a low flame. Place snappers in a baking pan. Add salt and pepper and brush snappers with melted butter. Place in oven for 10 minutes. Remove from oven, pour sauce over the snappers, and serve. *Serves* 6

Crawfish Newburg
BON TON

2 pounds crawfish tail meat	½ teaspoon salt
2 sticks butter	½ teaspoon black pepper
2 cups Cream Sauce II (p. 235)	2 tablespoons sherry

Sauté crawfish meat in butter. Add cream sauce, salt, pepper, and sherry. Simmer about 10 minutes. Serve over Holland Rusk. *Serves* 4

Crawfish Étouffée
LEAH CHASE

1 cup butter	Salt and pepper to taste
5 cups crawfish tails, cleaned	Water as necessary
1 tablespoon fat from head of crawfish*	

Melt butter in saucepan and add crawfish. Let cook until all juices have evaporated. Add fat from crawfish heads. Add salt and pepper and just enough water to make a thick but soupy mixture. Cook slowly for half an hour. Serve over steamed rice. *Serves* 4

* This fat can be purchased from seafood dealers. It is available in one-pound packages. In the head of a crawfish, it is easily identified by its yellow color.

Soft-Shell Crabs
AUSTIN LESLIE

6 medium-sized, soft-shell
  crabs, cleaned
1 cup flour
Egg Wash (p. 107)

1 cup commercial fish fry (see
  Glossary, p. 315)
Oil for frying

Roll crabs in flour, then in egg wash, then in fish fry. Heat oil in frying pan and brown crabs evenly, allowing 10 minutes on each side (20 minutes in all). *Serves* 3

Stuffed Crabs
NATHANIEL BURTON

4 ounces butter
1 onion, minced
2 ribs celery, finely chopped
2 tablespoons fresh parsley,
  chopped
1 green bell pepper, finely
  chopped

1½ pounds fresh lump
  crabmeat
2 cups fresh Breadcrumbs
  (p. 267)
1 tablespoon salt
1 teaspoon cayenne
1 dozen aluminum crab shells

Preheat oven to 400°. Melt butter in skillet. Add onion, celery, parsley, and green pepper and cook until tender. Add crabmeat, cook about 5 minutes. Stir in 1 cup of the breadcrumbs, salt, and cayenne. Mix and cook 5 minutes. Stuff shells with crab mixture. Sprinkle with remaining breadcrumbs and bake for 10 minutes. *Serves* 6

Crabmeat au Gratin I
MALCOM ROSS

1½ pounds fresh crabmeat
1 green onion, finely chopped
2 tablespoons fresh parsley,
  finely chopped
1½ cups Cream Sauce II (¼ of
  recipe) (p. 235)

2 ounces Fish Stock (p. 214)
3 egg yolks
1 cup breadcrumbs
¼ cup grated parmesan
  cheese (optional)
¼ pound butter, melted

Preheat broiler or oven. Combine crabmeat, onion, parsley, cream sauce, and fish stock in a saucepan. Heat slowly over medium heat, then add egg yolks and stir gently until blended. Put mixture into individual casseroles. Sprinkle breadcrumbs (and cheese, if desired) on top and pour butter over each dish. Place in broiler until crumbs are brown or in a 350° oven for 5 minutes. *Serves* 4

Crabmeat au Gratin II
BON TON

1 pound fresh lump crabmeat
2 tablespoons fresh mush-
  rooms, sliced
3 tablespoons sherry

1 cup American cheese,
  grated
1½ cups Cream Sauce II
  (p. 235)

Preheat open grill. Mix together crabmeat, mushrooms, sherry, and grated cheese. Blend in cream sauce. Put crabmeat mixture in individual casseroles and sprinkle additional grated cheese on top. Place casseroles on top of a hot open grill and cook for 10 minutes. Then place under broiler until cheese is bubbly. *Serves* 4

Crabmeat Imperial I
BON TON

1 bunch green onions, chopped
½ pound butter
1 cup olive oil
1 pound fresh lump crabmeat
1 tablespoon chopped pimento

¼ cup fresh mushrooms, sliced
Salt and pepper to taste
1 tablespoon sherry
Toast points

Sauté green onions in butter about 5 minutes. Add olive oil, crabmeat, pimento, mushrooms, salt, and pepper and sauté an additional 5 minutes. Add sherry and serve on toast points. *Serves* 4

Crabmeat Imperial II
RAYMOND THOMAS, SR.

1 bunch green onions, chopped
1 small can pimentos, chopped
1 small can mushrooms
    (stems and pieces) or ¼ cup
    fresh mushrooms, chopped

1 tablespoon dry mustard
2 cups Mayonnaise (p. 244, or
    use ready-made)
2 pounds lump crabmeat

Preheat oven to 350°. Place onions, pimentos, and mushrooms in a large bowl. Add mustard and mayonnaise and fold ingredients together, adding crabmeat last. Place in casserole and put in 350° oven for 10 minutes or until brown. *Serves 4 to* 6

Crabmeat Newburg
MALCOM ROSS

1½ pounds fresh crabmeat
2 cups Cream Sauce II (1/4 of recipe, p. 235)
2 tablespoons sherry
2 egg yolks, beaten

Mix together crabmeat, cream sauce, and sherry, and heat. Stir in egg yolks just before serving. *Serves* 4

Crabmeat St. Pierre
MALCOM ROSS

1 pound fresh lump crabmeat
3 fresh whole tomatoes,
   peeled* and cut in wedges
3 stalks green onion, chopped
1 teaspoon garlic, minced
1 teaspoon fresh parsley,
   chopped
½ cup fresh mushrooms,
   sliced
Salt and pepper to taste

Place all ingredients in a skillet and simmer over medium flame for 15 minutes or until tomatoes are cooked. *Serves* 4 *to* 6

* To peel tomatoes, dip in hot oil for a few seconds. The skin will loosen immediately.

Crabmeat Far Horizon

LOUIS EVANS

1 cup cream sauce (see below)
½ cup Louis Evans's
   Hollandaise Sauce (p. 240)
1 tablespoon dry mustard
½ teaspoon curry powder
2 pounds lump crabmeat,
   drained
½ cup breadcrumbs

Cream Sauce
¼ stick butter
2 tablespoons flour
2 cups milk, scalded
Salt
1 cup water
1 egg yolk

For cream sauce, melt butter in saucepan. Add flour and stir. Add hot milk, salt, and water. Beat the egg yolk in last. Cook over low heat 5 to 10 minutes, or until creamy.

Preheat oven to 450°. Blend cream sauce, hollandaise, mustard, and curry powder thoroughly. Place crabmeat on ovenproof plates or in baking shells and cover with sauce mixture. Top with breadcrumbs and bake for 15 minutes. *Serves 6 to 8*

Baked Crabmeat and Avocado

HENRY CARR

¼ pound butter
2 cans cream of mushroom
   soup
1 pound lump crabmeat
1 cup evaporated milk

Salt and pepper to taste
2 avocados
2 teaspoons breadcrumbs
1 small can anchovies

Preheat oven to 350°. Melt butter and set aside 2 tablespoons. Add soup to remaining butter and simmer 5 minutes. Add crabmeat, milk, salt, and pepper and simmer 5 minutes longer. Peel and slice avocados. Line a baking dish with the slices. Pour crabmeat mixture over avocado slices, sprinkle with breadcrumbs and the

2 tablespoons of melted butter. Bake until brown, approximately 15 minutes. Before serving, sprinkle a few drops of anchovy oil on top and garnish with strips of anchovy. *Serves 4 to 6*

Crabmeat Lafitte
RAYMOND THOMAS, SR.

1 stick butter
2 tablespoons flour
2 cups milk
½ bunch green onions, finely chopped

1 pound fresh lump crabmeat
½ cup breadcrumbs
2 tablespoons grated parmesan cheese

Preheat oven to 350°. Melt butter in pan and add flour to make a roux. Stir for 5 minutes. Gradually add the milk, then the green onions. Fold in crabmeat and breadcrumbs. Top with cheese, put in casserole, and bake until brown, about 15 minutes. *Serves 4*

Crabmeat Yvonne
MALCOM ROSS

1½ pounds fresh crabmeat
4 cooked artichoke bottoms, sliced
½ cup fresh mushrooms, sliced
4 tablespoons butter

Sauté crabmeat, artichoke bottoms, and mushrooms in butter for 5 minutes. *Serves 4*

Crabmeat Ravigote
MALCOM ROSS

1½ pounds fresh lump
   crabmeat
½ stalk green onion, chopped
1 tablespoon fresh parsley,
   chopped

1½ cups Cream Sauce II (¼ of
   recipe) (p. 235)
½ cup Hollandaise Sauce II
   (p. 239)

Combine all ingredients in a saucepan, except the hollandaise sauce. Heat on low flame. When you are ready to serve, fold in hollandaise and stir gently until mixed. *Serves* 4

Olive Crab Mousse
ROCHESTER ANDERSON

½ cup canned pitted ripe
   black olives
5-ounce package frozen (or
   ½ pound fresh) asparagus
   spears
1 envelope unflavored gelatin
½ cup cold water
¼ cup Mayonnaise (p. 244 or
   use ready-made)
1 tablespoon lemon juice

½ teaspoon salt
¼ teaspoon Worcestershire
   sauce
¼ teaspoon Tabasco sauce
1 tablespoon ketchup
1 cup sour cream
4 ounces crabmeat
Salad greens
Tiny pickled green tomatoes

Slice olives. Cook asparagus just until tender, drain, and set aside. Sprinkle gelatin over water in a small pot and stir over low heat until dissolved. Put mayonnaise in a bowl and add the gelatin mixture to it, beating briskly. Blend in lemon juice, salt, Worcestershire, Tabasco, and ketchup. Set aside ½ the olives and ½ asparagus spears for mold. Chop remaining asparagus into discs and fold into gelatin mixture with the remaining olives, sour cream, and crabmeat. Chill until slightly thickened. Place reserved olives in bottom of a 6-cup mold. Cover with a little of the thickened gelatin mixture. Arrange asparagus spears, tips down, against sides of mold. Chill quickly, then spoon in remaining gelatin mixture. Chill until firm. Unmold on salad greens and garnish with green tomatoes. *Serves 6*

Pan-Roasted Oysters
MALCOM ROSS

1 stick butter, melted	Salt and pepper to taste
½ cup flour	4 tablespoons breadcrumbs
1 pint oyster soup	1 tablespoon fresh chopped
4 dozen oysters	parsley

Preheat oven to 400°. Melt ½ the butter and mix it with the flour in a saucepan over medium heat, to make a roux. Add oyster soup, oysters, and salt and pepper. Cook until slightly thickened (approximately 3 minutes). Put into individual casseroles, top with breadcrumbs, parsley, and remaining butter. Put in warmer or in a 400° oven for 5 minutes. *Serves 4 to 6*

Oysters Carnaval
CORINNE DUNBAR'S

2 dozen raw oysters	½ bay leaf, crumbled
7 tablespoons butter	Pinch of thyme
1¼ large or 2 small onions, minced	¾ cup breadcrumbs
	6 clean oyster shells
1 small clove garlic, minced	6 strips crisp-fried bacon
2 celery ribs, finely chopped	6 lemon wedges

Chop oysters and let them drain, saving the liquid. In 3 tablespoons of the butter, sauté the onion, garlic, celery, bay leaf, and thyme in an iron skillet until brown. Add the chopped oysters.

Moisten ½ cup of the breadcrumbs with the oyster liquid and add to the oyster mixture. Simmer for 20 to 30 minutes, or until oysters have stopped drawing water. Add 2 tablespoons of the butter and cook until butter is melted.

Boil and scrub the oyster shells. Fill the oyster shells with oyster mixture, sprinkle with remaining breadcrumbs, and dot with remaining butter. When ready to serve, put in a 375° oven for a few minutes until thoroughly heated. Serve at once, garnished with bacon pieces and lemon wedges. *Serves* 6

Oysters Caribbean

NATHANIEL BURTON

4 green onions, chopped
4 tablespoons butter
1 quart oysters, drained
1 tablespoon parsley, finely
    chopped

2 teaspoons Worcestershire
    sauce
2 cups Cream Sauce I (p. 234)
6 cups hot steamed rice

Sauté onions in butter about 8 minutes. Brown oysters in lightly greased, very heavy skillet or griddle. When brown, add to onions and simmer. Add parsley, Worcestershire, and cream sauce. Simmer at least 10 minutes. Serve with hot rice. *Serves* 6

Oysters Louisiana
RAYMOND THOMAS, SR.

4 ounces butter, melted
1½ pints oysters, drained
4 green onions, finely
   chopped

3 cloves garlic, minced
½ pound fresh lump crabmeat
½ cup breadcrumbs
Salt and pepper to taste

Melt butter in a skillet. Add oysters and cook until dry. Add onions and garlic and cook slowly for at least 10 minutes. Fold in crabmeat and breadcrumbs. Simmer 5 minutes more. Add salt and pepper to taste. *Serves* 4

Crab Oyster Pan Roast
HENRY CARR

2 cups milk
2 cups oyster water (saved
   from oysters)
2 sticks margarine
½ cup flour
6 shallots or 2 bunches of
   green onions, finely chopped
½ white onion, finely chopped

1 bunch parsley, finely
   chopped
4 dozen small oysters
1 pound fresh lump crabmeat
2 tablespoons Worcestershire
   sauce
1 teaspoon Tabasco sauce
1 cup breadcrumbs

Bring milk and oyster water to a boil in a half-gallon pot. Melt margarine in a skillet and combine with flour to make a roux. Cook 5 minutes. Add milk and oyster water to the roux and stir in the chopped vegetables. Poach oysters in water barely enough to cover them until edges curl. Remove from pan and mix with crabmeat. Add sauce and cook 3 minutes. Add Worcestershire sauce and Tabasco. Fill eight individual casseroles with 6 oysters each. Cover with sauce and sprinkle with breadcrumbs. Dot with margarine. Place under broiler until golden brown. *Serves* 8

Breast of Turkey and Oysters Supreme

NATHANIEL BURTON

2 dozen oysters
1 cup water and 1 cup
   Chicken Stock (p. 213) or 2
   cups water
3 green onions, chopped
4 ounces butter
4 tablespoons flour
8 fresh mushrooms, sliced

1½ cups cooked turkey breast,
   diced
2 cups Cream Sauce I (p. 234)
Salt and pepper
2 pimentos, diced
1 tablespoon fresh parsley,
   chopped

Bring oysters to boil in the cup of water. Remove from stove, but leave in water. In a saucepan, sauté onions in the butter until tender. Add flour to the onions and blend to make a roux. Cook slowly about 5 minutes. Stir in the oysters and their liquid. Simmer on a very low flame for 5 minutes.

In a separate pot, add the cup of chicken stock (or water) to mushrooms and turkey. Simmer for 3 or 4 minutes. Add cream sauce to the turkey mixture and stir thoroughly. Combine oyster mixture and turkey mixture. Add salt, pepper, pimentos, and chopped parsley. *Serves* 6

Shrimp Étouffée

BON TON

1 tablespoon butter
1 cup fresh small shrimp,
   peeled and deveined
Dash of salt and pepper

¼ teaspoon garlic, minced
1 teaspoon chopped fresh
   parsley

Melt butter in a small skillet. Add shrimp, salt, pepper, and garlic. Cook about 10 minutes. Add parsley. Serve with parsley-buttered rice. *Serves* 1

Shrimp Clemenceau I

LEAH CHASE

1 stick butter
2 medium potatoes, peeled
   and diced small
2 pounds small shrimp (fresh
   or uncooked, if frozen),
   peeled and deveined
2 cloves garlic, finely chopped
½ cup button mushrooms
   (fresh or canned)

1 cup green peas (if fresh peas
   are used, precook them)
¼ teaspoon fresh chopped
   parsley
⅓ cup white wine
Salt and pepper to taste

Melt butter in 2-quart saucepan. Add potatoes and cook for 5 minutes. Add shrimp, garlic, and mushrooms and cook until shrimp are tender. Add peas, parsley, wine, salt, and pepper and cook about 5 minutes. *Serves 4 to 6*

Shrimp Clemenceau II

MALCOM ROSS

½ pound potatoes (2
   medium-sized)
Oil for frying
2 pounds small cooked shrimp

½ pound fresh mushrooms,
   sliced
1 stick butter, melted
1 tablespoon garlic, minced

Peel and dice potatoes. Deep-fry in oil for 10 minutes at 360°. Sauté the shrimps and mushrooms in the butter. When hot, add potatoes and garlic and serve. *Serves 6*

Shrimp Clemenceau III
SHERMAN CRAYTON

1 pound fresh medium-sized
   shrimp, peeled and deveined
½ stick margarine
1 cup fresh mushrooms, sliced

1 medium potato, diced
1 cup green peas
2 cloves garlic, minced
Salt and pepper to taste

Sauté shrimp in margarine for 5 minutes. Add remaining ingredients and cook until the potatoes are done. *Serves* 4

Shrimp Creole I
SHERMAN CRAYTON

1 pound fresh medium-sized
   shrimp, peeled and
   deveined
1 stick butter
3 green bell peppers (cut in
   large sections or sliced)
3 medium white onions, sliced

1 rib celery, sliced
1 #3 can whole tomatoes,
   crushed
Pinch of thyme
2 bay leaves
2 garlic cloves (crushed)
Salt and pepper to taste

Sauté shrimp in butter for 10 minutes. Add peppers, onions, and celery and cook for another 10 minutes, then stir in the tomatoes, thyme, bay leaves, and crushed garlic. Add salt and pepper to taste and cook for another 10 minutes. Serve over rice. *Serves* 3

Shrimp Creole II
LEAH CHASE

4 tablespoons vegetable
  shortening
5 tablespoons flour
½ cup chopped onion
3 cloves garlic, minced
¼ cup green bell pepper,
  chopped
¼ cup celery, chopped

1 8-ounce can tomato sauce
  (or 1 cup Basic Tomato
  Sauce, p. 237)
3 cups water
½ teaspoon salt
¼ teaspoon cayenne pepper
3 pounds fresh shrimp,
  medium or jumbo, cleaned
  and deveined

Melt shortening in a 2-quart saucepan. Add flour and cook over a medium flame, stirring constantly to make a golden-brown roux. Add onion, garlic, green pepper, and celery and cook until tender. Add tomato sauce. Stir and cook about 5 minutes. Add water, salt, and cayenne. Simmer for 15 minutes. Add shrimp. Cover and simmer for 20 minutes more. Serve over rice. *Serves* 6

Shrimp à la Poulette
MALCOM ROSS

2 pounds cooked shrimp
2 cups Cream Sauce II (p. 235)
½ cup fresh mushrooms,
  sliced if large

1 ounce sherry
3 egg yolks

Put shrimp, cream sauce, mushrooms, and sherry in pan. Stir gently. When mixture is hot, add egg yolks. Stir until completely mixed. *Serves* 4

Fried Shrimp
LEAH CHASE

1 egg
1 cup cold water
Salt and pepper
2 pounds fresh shrimp
  (peeled and deveined)

2 cups corn flour (see
  Glossary, p. 315)
2 cups vegetable oil

Beat egg slightly with fork. Add water, mix well. Salt and pepper shrimp. Dip shrimp in egg mixture, then roll in corn flour until well coated. Cook in hot oil until light brown. Drain on paper towel. *Serves 6*

Scampi Conti
CHARLES BAILEY

1 egg
1 cup milk
Salt and white pepper to taste
3 pounds large fresh shrimp
  (10-to-15-count per pound)
¼ cup flour, or more as
  necessary
5 ounces vegetable oil

¼ stick butter
½ pound fresh mushrooms,
  sliced
1 bunch green onions,
  chopped
½ cup fresh pineapple chunks
2 ounces white wine

Beat egg and combine with milk, salt, and pepper to make a batter. Dip shrimp in batter, dust very lightly with flour, and then sauté in the combined oil and butter for 6 minutes over medium flame. Do not let shrimp brown. Add mushrooms, onions, and pineapple. Reduce heat and cook for 4 minutes, then add wine. Serve with Rice Pilaf (p. 197). *Serves 6*

Shrimp 21

LOUIS EVANS

1½ pounds fresh shrimp, peeled and deveined

2 cups water (or Shrimp Stock [p. 213])

½ bunch green onions, chopped

6 fresh mushrooms, sliced

1 stick butter

¼ cup flour

2 ounces sherry

2 ounces Sauterne

4 ounces half-and-half

Salt and pepper to taste

6 medium-sized pastry shells

Bring shrimp to boil in 2 cups water or stock for 5 minutes, until half-cooked. Remove them from water and set aside. Sauté green onions and mushrooms in butter for 5 to 8 minutes. Add flour and stir. Do not brown. Then add stock, plus the shrimp, sherry, and Sauterne and stir together. Heat cream and add to shrimp mixture slowly. Add salt and pepper and cook mixture about 30 minutes, or until creamy. Place mixture in pastry shells and serve with fresh asparagus. *Serves* 6

Shrimp Marguery

LARRY WILLIAMSON

3 pounds raw shrimp, shells intact

1 tablespoon cayenne pepper

2 tablespoons salt

1 16-ounce can mushrooms or 1 pound fresh mushrooms, sliced

2 cups Cream Sauce II (p. 235)

2 cups Hollandaise Sauce II (p. 239, or use ready-made)

In a deep pot, bring shrimp to a boil in 8 inches of water. Add cayenne and salt. Boil 8 to 10 minutes. Drain, cool, peel, and devein shrimp. Combine mushrooms with cream sauce and hollandaise. If you are using fresh mushrooms, you may want to sauté them briefly in a little butter before adding to the sauce. Stir the sauce over a low flame for 5 to 8 minutes, or until hot. Add shrimp. Stir for another minute. *Serves 6 to 8*

Stuffed Shrimp I

NATHANIEL BURTON

2 green onions, finely chopped
1 celery rib, finely chopped
½ green bell pepper, finely chopped
2 cloves garlic, minced
3 ounces butter
1 pound fresh claw crabmeat
4 cups breadcrumbs
1 tablespoon parsley, chopped
Salt and pepper to taste
2 pounds fresh fantail shrimp (12-to-15-count per pound)
1 cup flour
Egg Wash (p. 107)
Oil for frying

Sauté all vegetables in butter until tender. Add crabmeat and mix well. Add one tablespoon of the breadcrumbs and the parsley. Season with salt and pepper. Set aside. Clean shrimp and peel down to fantail. Split and devein. Fill each shrimp with crab dressing. Roll in flour, dip in egg wash, then roll shrimp in remaining breadcrumbs. Deep-fry in oil about 5 minutes. Drain and serve. *Serves 6*

Stuffed Shrimp II

AUSTIN LESLIE

3 pounds (about 36) fresh
   jumbo shrimp, with fantails
Salt and pepper
2 cups flour
Egg Wash (p. 107)
1 box commercial fish fry (see
   Glossary, p. 315)
Oil for frying

Crabmeat Dressing
1 stick margarine (or 3 ounces
   of butter)
4 sprigs parsley, finely
   chopped
1 celery rib, finely chopped
1 whole onion, finely chopped
1 pound crabmeat
1 loaf French bread
2 eggs
Salt and pepper to taste

Preheat oven to 350°. To make dressing: Melt margarine in skillet with parsley, celery, and onion and sauté for 10 to 15 minutes. Add crabmeat and sauté for an additional 10 to 15 minutes. While crabmeat sautés, moisten bread (it should be wet but not soggy) in a bowl and then chop it. Add eggs and mix. Add crabmeat mixture to bread and eggs. Season with salt and pepper. Place in a baking pan and bake for 1 hour. Stir after the first ½ hour of cooking. Remove from oven and place in refrigerator and cool to refrigerator temperature (approximately 45°).

   Peel shrimp, making sure to leave on fantails. Devein shrimp and sprinkle them with salt and pepper. Take dressing from refrigerator. For each shrimp, place 1 tablespoon of dressing in palm of hand, spread evenly to ⅛ inch thick. Place shrimp in dressing, roll and pat well. Roll shrimp in flour, then in egg wash, then in fish fry. Place in frying pan and brown evenly by moving shrimp around for 10 minutes on each side (20 minutes in all).
Serves 6

Shrimp Marinière I

SHERMAN CRAYTON

1 pound fresh shrimp, peeled
  and deveined
1 stick butter
3 tablespoons flour
1 cup green onions, chopped

½ cup fresh parsley, chopped
2 cloves garlic, minced
4 cups water
½ cup white wine

Sauté shrimp in butter for 4 minutes. Remove from pan and set aside. Add flour to the butter in the pan and stir for approximately 5 minutes to make a white roux. Be careful not to let it brown or burn. Remember, the sauce is not a dark sauce; it's light. Add onions, parsley, and garlic. Continue to sauté for approximately 3 to 4 minutes, then add water and cook for 5 minutes more. Return shrimp to the pan and, on a low flame, cook for about 15 minutes. Add wine and stir before removing from heat. This dish should not be served over rice. *Serves* 4

Shrimp Marinière II

LOUIS EVANS

1½ pounds fresh shrimp
2 cups white wine
2 minced shallots or green
  onions or ¼ cup minced
  white onion
1 cup oyster water, Fish Stock
  (p. 214), Shrimp Stock
  (p. 213), or Chicken Stock
  (p. 213)

2 tablespoons butter
2 tablespoons flour
Juice of ¼ lemon
2 egg yolks
½ cup light cream
1 tablespoon fresh parsley,
  chopped

Peel and devein shrimp. Combine wine, shallots, and oyster water (or stock). Bring to a boil, then simmer about 15 minutes.

Melt butter and blend in flour. Gradually add ¾ cup of the wine-oyster water to roux, stirring constantly until thickened. Add shrimp and cook 10 minutes, then add lemon juice. Beat egg yolks and mix with cream. Combine with hot shrimp mixture, stirring constantly. Serve on toast points or in ramekins garnished with parsley. *Serves* 6

Stewed Shrimp
NATHANIEL BURTON

2 pounds fresh medium-size shrimp, peeled and deveined
4 ounces butter
1 green bell pepper, finely chopped
1 onion, finely chopped
2 cloves garlic, minced

1 bay leaf
Pinch of thyme
4 tablespoons flour
1½ pints of Shrimp Stock (p. 213)
Salt to taste
Cayenne pepper to taste
Dash of soy sauce

Bring shrimp to a boil in 2 quarts of water. Drain shrimp and set aside. Reserve shrimp stock. Put butter in 2-quart saucepan. Sauté green pepper and onion in the butter until tender. Add garlic, bay leaf, thyme and, bit by bit, the flour. Blend well. Add stock slowly, stirring constantly. Season with salt, cayenne, and soy sauce. Cook about 10 minutes and then add shrimp. Cook 10 minutes longer. Serve with rice. *Serves* 5

Scampi Butter
ROCHESTER ANDERSON

1¼ cups butter
1 tablespoon shallots or green onions, chopped
2 cloves garlic, crushed

½ tablespoon parsley, finely chopped
1 tablespoon salt and a little pepper

Soften butter at room temperature. Add green onions, garlic, and parsley and mix with butter, salt, and pepper. Chill until ready to use.

Scampi Provençale
ROCHESTER ANDERSON

2 pounds shrimp in shell	2 cups Scampi Butter (p. 152)
Salt and pepper	Juice of 4 lemons
Dash of paprika	

Preheat broiler to 350°. Shell the shrimp, but be careful not to remove tail. Devein shrimp and place in a shallow ovenproof baking dish large enough to hold them in one layer. Salt and pepper to taste and sprinkle with paprika. Brush shrimp with scampi butter and lemon juice. Put under broiler for approximately 15 minutes or until cooked, brushing them often with scampi butter and lemon juice. Be careful not to let shrimp overcook. Transfer shrimp and any melted butter left in pan to a hot serving plate. Pour on remaining butter and serve immediately. *Serves* 6

Stuffed Lobster
AUSTIN LESLIE

3 live Florida or Maine lobsters	¼ cup breadcrumbs
1 box commercial seafood seasoning	2 ounces margarine, melted
Salt and pepper to taste	6 lemon slices
1 teaspoon cayenne pepper	½ clove garlic, finely chopped
1 lemon, sliced	4 sprigs parsley, chopped
1 recipe Crabmeat Dressing (p. 150)	Dash of paprika

Put lobsters in large pot of boiling water along with seafood seasoning, salt and pepper, cayenne, and sliced lemon. Make sure water covers the lobsters. Cover pot and bring water back to boiling. Turn flame off, remove lobsters, and let them sit for 5 minutes before placing in refrigerator to cool. When cool, cut lobsters in half. Clean the heads and devein the tails. Stuff heads with crabmeat dressing and pack well. Cover dressing with breadcrumbs. Sprinkle melted margarine on each lobster half. Place under broiler for 10 minutes. Before serving, place slice of lemon on each lobster half, top with garlic and parsley and a sprinkling of paprika. *Serves 6 (½ lobster each)*

Lobster Armorican
CHARLES BAILEY

3 live Maine or Florida
　lobsters
3 raw carrots, diced (do not
　peel)
½ rib celery, chopped
½ bunch fresh parsley, chopped
½ Bermuda onion, sliced
2 bay leaves
½ teaspoon ground black
　peppercorns
½ teaspoon paprika
1 ounce butter
10 ounces cooking oil
2 tablespoons flour
　(all-purpose)

2 cups Shellfish Stock (p. 213)
3 ounces brandy
Salt and pepper to taste
1 cup whipping cream

Lobster Béarnaise Sauce
6 egg yolks
5 ounces hot or lukewarm
　water
1½ pounds clarified butter
　(see Glossary, p. 315)
½ ounce fresh tarragon leaves
10 ounces red wine
2 whole tomatoes, chopped

Split lobsters in half down the middle. If you are using Maine lobsters, disjoint the claws from body and crack claws in several places before using. Do not remove green particles. Also, with a Maine lobster, remove the fat and reserve. A Florida lobster has no fat. When using a Florida lobster, remove entrails before cooking. Put all vegetables and seasonings, together with the butter and oil, in a large heavy pot. Cook over medium-high flame for 8 to 9 minutes, stirring constantly. Place lobsters (in their shells) into pot of vegetables. Shake lobsters around in the vegetables and continue to cook until they turn red (approximately 10 to 15 minutes). Remove lobsters from pot and place on a serving dish.

Prepare brandy sauce as follows: Add flour and the fat from the Maine lobster to the pot vegetables. Stir for 5 minutes. Add stock, brandy, salt, and pepper to taste. Remove from fire and strain thoroughly. Return strained sauce to flame for 5 minutes, then add whipping cream. Reserve.

Prepare Lobster Béarnaise Sauce as follows: Place egg yolks and 2 ounces of the water in a stainless-steel mixing bowl. Place over double boiler and whip until fluffy. Remove from double boiler. Add butter to egg mixture and whip thoroughly. Set aside. Place tarragon leaves in saucepan with wine and 3 ounces of the water. Cook over a low flame for 6 minutes until reduced. Remove from heat, strain, and save the juice. Chop the wine-soaked tarragon leaves into tiny pieces. Place in frying pan with tomatoes and butter or oil. Sauté for 2 or 3 minutes. Mix the tarragon, tomatoes, and the wine juice into the egg mixture. Place in a separate dish and serve on the side as a dip for lobster. Serve with rice topped with brandy sauce. *Serves* 6

Frogs' Legs
AUSTIN LESLIE

6 frogs' legs, separated at joint
1 cup flour
Egg Wash (p. 107)

1 cup commercial fish fry (see Glossary, p. 315)
Oil for frying

Roll frogs' legs in flour, dip in egg wash, then in fish fry. Heat oil in frying pan. Add frogs' legs and brown evenly for 10 minutes on each side (20 minutes in all), being sure to move them around. *Serves* 3

Frogs' Legs Sans Souci
RAYMOND THOMAS, SR.

3 pounds frogs' legs
1 cup flour
1 cup olive oil

5 cloves garlic, chopped
Juice of ½ lemon
Salt and pepper to taste

Lightly dust frogs' legs in flour. Put olive oil and garlic in a skillet and heat. Add frogs' legs. Squeeze lemon juice over preparation and sauté for 10 minutes. Season with salt and pepper. *Serves* 6

MEATS

Country Ham

ROCHESTER ANDERSON

1 16-pound fresh smoked ham
Tea solution, enough to cover
  ham
1 pound raisins

2 apples, cut up
1 pound brown sugar
½ cup cloves
1 cup dry white wine

Preheat oven to 350°. Scrub ham thoroughly and soak overnight in strong tea. Put ham in roasting pan ¼ full of water and add raisins and apples. Put in oven and cook for 4 hours or about 20 minutes per pound, basting with fruit and juices every 15 minutes. Remove from pan, skin, and cover with brown sugar. Stick ham with whole cloves and place in a clean pan. Pour wine over ham and cook for 1 hour, basting every 15 minutes with the wine.

Baked Ham

NATHANIEL BURTON

1 14-pound precooked ham,
  with bone left in
½ cup brown sugar
½ cup dry mustard

1 small can sliced pineapple
1 12-ounce can pineapple
  juice

Preheat oven to 450°. Trim skin and fat from ham and place in roasting pan. Mix sugar and mustard and rub the mixture into the ham, coating thoroughly. Bake in oven until brown. Place pineapple slices on ham with toothpicks and pour the pineapple juice over it. Reduce the oven temperature to 350° and cook at least 1½ hours more. Skim fat from juices in pan and serve. *Serves* 15

Ham Steak with Apple Jelly

NATHANIEL BURTON

2 tablespoons butter
1 10-to 12- ounce center cut ham steak
¼ cup apple jelly
5 ounces sherry

Melt butter in skillet and add ham. Brown on both sides. Remove ham to warm platter. Add jelly and wine to skillet. Let the jelly melt with the wine, stir gently, and pour over the ham steak. *Serves* 2

Center Cut Pork Chops Lyonnaise

NATHANIEL BURTON

4 tablespoons shortening
5 center cut loin pork chops
1 tablespoon flour

½ cup Brown Gravy I (p. 233)
4 tablespoons butter
2 large onions, sliced

Preheat oven to 350°. Melt shortening in skillet. Dredge chops in flour, put in skillet, and brown on both sides. Pour off excess fat. Remove chops from skillet, put in casserole, and pour the brown gravy over them. Place in preheated oven. Melt the butter in a saucepan, add onions, and brown. As soon as onions are done, add them to the pork chops, cover, and cook for at least 30 minutes. *Serves* 5

Stuffed Pork Chops I
NATHANIEL BURTON

4 ounces butter
1 medium onion, finely chopped
½ green bell pepper, finely chopped
2 dozen oysters, chopped
1 teaspoon oregano
1 teaspoon thyme

1 teaspoon marjoram
Salt
Pepper
1½ cups diced French bread
6 double loin pork chops (have butcher cut a pocket in each)

Preheat oven to 400°. Melt butter in skillet and add onion and green pepper. Cook until tender. Add oysters, oregano, thyme, marjoram, salt, and pepper to taste. Cook 5 minutes, add the bread, and stir well to blend. Stuff the pork chops and place in a baking pan in preheated oven. Cook at least 45 minutes. *Serves* 6

Stuffed Pork Chops II
AUSTIN LESLIE

6 loin pork chops, center cut (have butcher cut a pocket in each)
Stuffing (follow recipe for Stuffed Peppers, p. 201)

4 ounces margarine
1 cup water
1 cup Brown Gravy II (p. 233)

Preheat oven to 350°. Stuff pork chops with filling and close pockets with heavy toothpicks. Place in baking pan and pour melted margarine over the top of each chop. Add approximately 1 inch of water to the pan and place it in preheated oven. Cook for 1½ hours, turning after 45 minutes so that chops brown evenly on both sides. Cover with brown gravy before serving. *Serves* 6

Bar-b-que
AUSTIN LESLIE

8 pounds pork spareribs
(2 slabs)
Salt
Pepper
½ cup commercial smoke
flavoring (see Glossary,
p. 318)
6 cups water

¼ pound margarine
1 rib celery, chopped
1 onion, chopped
4 sprigs parsley, chopped
1 cup flour
1 can tomato paste
2 teaspoons brown sugar

Preheat oven to 350°. Sprinkle the ribs with salt and pepper and with some of the smoke flavoring. Put ribs in baking dish with 2 cups of water. Bake for 1½ to 2 hours, turning ribs occasionally so as to brown on all sides. Remove and set aside.

Melt margarine in large pot and add the chopped vegetables. Sauté lightly and simmer until tender. Add flour, tomato paste, smoke flavoring, and brown sugar and sauté for 20 minutes. Add water (approximately 4 cups) to half fill the pot and cook for 1 hour. If sauce is too thick, thin with a little water or drippings from ribs in baking pan. Drain drippings from meat in pan and pour sauce over the ribs. Return to oven for 30 minutes to glaze. *Serves* 6

Baked Stuffed Lamb Chops
NATHANIEL BURTON

¼ cup butter
3 green onions, finely
chopped
½ green bell pepper, finely
chopped

½ cup ham, finely chopped
½ breadcrumbs
6 double French cut rib lamb
chops

Preheat oven to 400°. Melt butter in skillet and sauté onions and green pepper until golden. Stir in ham and cook about 6 minutes. Add breadcrumbs and combine thoroughly. Stuff lamb chops with mixture. Place on a greased baking pan in the oven and cook for 15 to 20 minutes. *Serves 6*

Rack of Lamb Jacqueline
ROCHESTER ANDERSON

1 half rack of lamb (have butcher prepare for oven)
Salt
Pepper
1 branch fresh rosemary or 1 teaspoon dried rosemary
1 tablespoon parsley, finely chopped
1 clove garlic, minced
1 tablespoon dry breadcrumbs
Mint sauce (p. 249) or mint jelly

Preheat oven to 375°. Season lamb with salt and pepper. Place on meat rack in shallow roasting pan and bake with the rosemary for 30 minutes or until tender. Combine parsley, garlic, and breadcrumbs. Sprinkle on top of lamb and cook for 5 minutes more. Serve with mint sauce or mint jelly. *Serves 2 to 3*

Boiled Shoulder of Lamb with Caper Sauce
NATHANIEL BURTON

2 lamb shoulders, boned and tied
1 onion
2 ribs celery
2 bay leaves
Salt
Pepper
Water
¼ pound butter
1 tablespoon flour
½ cup capers
¼ cup vinegar

In soup pot, combine lamb, onion, celery, bay leaves, salt, and pepper. Cover with cold water and bring to a boil. Skim and let simmer at least 2 hours. Melt butter in a saucepan, add flour, and combine to make a roux. Add 2 cups of the water in which the lamb has cooked, blend carefully, and add the capers and the vinegar. Taste for seasoning. To serve, slice lamb, top with caper sauce, and serve on a warm plate with boiled potatoes. *Serves* 8

Barbecued Leg of Lamb
NATHANIEL BURTON

6- to 7-pound leg of lamb	1 cup ketchup
2 ribs celery, diced	½ cup brown sugar
1 medium onion, diced	2 tablespoons chili powder
1 cup vinegar	½ cup pineapple juice

Preheat oven to 375°. Put lamb in roasting pan with celery and onion and roast for 2 hours. Mix rest of ingredients and baste lamb frequently with them during cooking. When lamb has cooled, slice and serve cold. *Serves 6 to* 8

Braised Lamb Chops Jardinière
NATHANIEL BURTON

6 loin lamb chops	1 #303 can #2 peas
4 ounces (1 stick) butter	3 potatoes, diced and fried
10 fresh mushrooms, sliced	Salt
1 #303 can Belgian carrots	Pepper

Preheat oven to 350°. Brown lamb chops in frying pan. Discard fat and place chops in large casserole. Melt the butter in a skillet and brown the mushroom slices. Add carrots, peas, and potatoes. Season with salt and pepper, toss lightly, and put in casserole with the lamb chops. Cover and bake for 30 minutes. *Serves* 6

Irish Lamb Stew
NATHANIEL BURTON

4 pounds boneless lamb stew
    meat, cut into 1-inch cubes
1 onion, finely chopped
2 ribs celery, finely chopped

3 medium potatoes, diced
Salt
Pepper
2 bay leaves

Put lamb, onion, and celery in stew pot. Cover with water. Cook uncovered at a low boil about 1¼ hours. Skim froth off top and add potatoes. Season with salt, pepper, and bay leaves. Let cook at least 10 minutes longer and serve. *Serves* 8

Entrecôte Burton
NATHANIEL BURTON

¼ pound butter
1 bunch green onions (½ cup
    finely chopped)
1 8-ounce bottle steak sauce
1 8-ounce bottle
    Worcestershire sauce

½ cup Beef Stock (p. 213)
6 8-ounce sirloin steaks,
    trimmed
Salt
Pepper

Melt butter in skillet. Add green onions and cook until tender. Combine steak sauce, Worcestershire, and beef stock and add to pan. Simmer about 10 minutes. Meanwhile in a separate skillet, pan-broil the steaks after rubbing them with butter. Sprinkle with salt and pepper. When steaks are done, spoon the sauce over them, turning well so that all sauce is absorbed. *Serves* 6

Swiss Steak à la Creole
NATHANIEL BURTON

6 tablespoons shortening
6 8-ounce steaks, cut from
  top round
1 tablespoon flour
1 onion, finely chopped

1 green bell pepper, finely
  chopped
2 cups Beef Stock (p. 213)
Salt
Pepper

Preheat oven to 350°. Melt shortening in heavy ovenproof skillet. Dredge meat in flour and brown in shortening on both sides. Remove meat from pan and add onion and green pepper. Cook until tender. Return the meat to the pan and add the beef stock. Season with salt and pepper. Cover and cook in oven for 45 minutes. *Serves* 6

Barbequed Sirloin Steak
NATHANIEL BURTON

3 tablespoons onion, finely
  chopped
1 clove garlic, minced
½ cup soy sauce
½ cup A-1 sauce
¼ cup Worcestershire sauce

¼ cup ketchup
1 tablespoon dry mustard
Salt
Pepper
1 sirloin steak, about 2 inches
  thick

Preheat oven broiler to 500°. Combine all ingredients, except the steak, to make a sauce and mix thoroughly. Brown steak rapidly under broiler. Remove from heat and place on piece of aluminum foil. Cover with sauce. Seal foil package carefully, place in baking pan and bake in preheated oven for 5 or 6 minutes. Serve hot with extra sauce on the side. *Serves* 4

London Broil
NATHANIEL BURTON

½ cup commercial pickling
spice (see Glossary, p. 317)
2 cups olive oil
Juice of 4 lemons
2 cups red wine
3 London broil steaks (or
flank steaks)

¼ cup butter
1 dozen fresh mushrooms,
sliced
2 cups Brown Gravy I (p. 233)

Combine pickling spice, olive oil, lemon juice, and 1½ cups wine. Marinate the meat for at least one day before cooking. Melt butter in a skillet. Add mushrooms and brown. Stir in brown gravy and ½ cup wine, blend well, and keep warm. Broil meat under medium heat. To serve, carve across the grain and pour the mushroom gravy over the slices. *Serves 6*

Daube Creole
CORINNE DUNBAR'S

3 bay leaves, crumbled fine
1 bunch fresh thyme, finely
chopped
4 whole cloves
1 bunch parsley, finely
chopped
3 cloves garlic, finely minced
2 large onions, finely chopped

2 tablespoons salt
1 tablespoon pepper
¼ pound salt pork fat, cut in
thin strips
12-14 pound boneless beef
round roast
3 quarts Beef Stock (p. 213)
2 cups sherry

Preheat oven to 300°. Combine bay leaves, thyme, cloves, parsley, garlic, and half the onion. Blend chopped vegetables with salt and pepper. Roll strips of salt pork in mixture. Make several incisions in beef roast and push seasoned salt pork in pockets. Sprinkle roast with rest of chopped onion. Brown roast in uncovered dry roasting pan for 30 minutes in oven. Pour beef stock and sherry over roast. Raise oven temperature to 350°. Cover pan and cook for 3½ hours. Slice and serve roast at table. (Guests should discard seasoned pork strips from their slices.) *Serves* 16 *to* 18

Broiled Kebabs
ROCHESTER ANDERSON

¼ cup olive oil
2 tablespoons lemon juice
1 teaspoon salt
¼ teaspoon pepper
4 bay leaves (whole)
Pinch thyme
Pinch rosemary

2 pounds lean beef or lamb, cut in 1½-inch cubes
1 pound medium white onions, peeled, whole
2 green bell peppers, cut in quarters

Heat broiler to 350°. Combine oil, lemon juice, and seasonings in bowl. Add meat and marinate several hours or overnight. Alternate pieces of meat, whole onions, and pepper quarters on skewers. Broil 10 to 15 minutes, turning occasionally. *Serves* 4

Braised Short Ribs of Beef
NATHANIEL BURTON

3 pounds lean short ribs
½ cup flour
½ cup onions, finely chopped
2 bay leaves
2½ cups water

4 large potatoes, peeled and diced
6 carrots, peeled and cut into diagonal slices
Salt and pepper

Preheat oven to 400°. Dredge short ribs in flour. Place in roasting pan and let brown in oven. Add onion and bay leaves and cook for at least 5 minutes. Add 2 cups water, reduce the oven temperature to 350°, cover pan, and cook for at least 1 hour. Add the potatoes, carrots, salt and pepper, and ½ cup water. Cook at least 20 minutes more. *Serves 6*

Pot Roast of Beef
NATHANIEL BURTON

½ cup shortening
6 pounds beef bottom round
1 cup flour
Salt
Pepper
1 onion, sliced

1 green bell pepper, sliced
2 ribs celery, diced
3 ripe tomatoes, chopped but
  not peeled
2 cups Beef Stock (p. 213)

Melt shortening in Dutch oven. Rub roast with flour, salt, and pepper. Brown on all sides. Remove roast from pot and add onion, green pepper, and celery. Allow vegetables to brown, then return roast to pot along with the tomatoes. Cover and cook very slowly for at least 2 hours, adding equal portions of the stock at half-hour intervals. *Serves 8*

Beef Tips à la Deutsch
RAYMOND THOMAS, SR.

1 cup cooking oil
2 pounds best-quality beef,
  cubed
1 cup flour
4 white onions, finely chopped

4 green bell peppers, finely
  chopped
1 clove garlic, finely minced
2 cups water

Heat oil in Dutch oven. Dredge beef cubes with flour and sauté in oil over medium heat until brown, about 15 minutes. Add all other ingredients except water and cook another 20 minutes.

Add water, cover, and cook until tender, about half an hour. Serve over long-grain rice. *Serves 4 to 6*

Beef Pot Pie with Biscuit Topping
NATHANIEL BURTON

½ cup shortening   2 ribs celery, chopped
4 pounds cubed beef   4 cups Beef Stock (p. 213)
2 tablespoons flour   4 carrots, diced
1 onion, chopped   8 prebaked biscuits

Preheat oven to 350°. Melt shortening in a Dutch oven or heavy skillet. Add beef and brown over medium-high flame. Stir in flour and let it brown. Add onion and celery and cook until tender. Add beef stock and reduce flame. Cook 10 minutes and add carrots. Simmer about 25 minutes. Pour into casserole and top with biscuits. Put in oven for no more than 3 to 4 minutes. *Serves 6 to 8*

Meat Loaf
NATHANIEL BURTON

1 onion, minced   2 eggs
4 tablespoons butter   ¼ cup milk
3 pounds ground beef   Salt
½ cup breadcrumbs   Pepper

Preheat oven to 375°. Sauté onion in butter until tender. When onion has cooled, combine with all other ingredients in mixing bowl and mix well. Shape meat mixture into loaf and bake for at least 1 hour. *Serves 6*

Grillades

CORINNE DUNBAR'S

1 tablespoon shortening
6 beef sirloin steaks, cut into
   6-inch squares ½-inch thick
   (veal or beef round may be
   substituted)
1 tablespoon flour
1 onion, chopped
1 clove garlic, chopped

4 sprigs thyme, chopped
2 bay leaves
1 green bell pepper, chopped
4 sprigs parsley, chopped
2 tomatoes, chopped
2 cups water
Salt
Pepper

Melt shortening in saucepan and brown beef. Remove from skillet and set aside. Add flour and all other ingredients except the last four to fat in pan and brown thoroughly to make a roux. Add the tomatoes, water, salt, and pepper. Simmer mixture about half an hour and then return the beef to the skillet and simmer until meat is tender. Serve grillades with gravy. *Serves* 6

Sautéed Veal à la Lemon

LOUIS EVANS

1½ pounds veal, sliced ⅜th of
   an inch thick and pounded
   thin
3 tablespoons flour
2 tablespoons butter
6 tablespoons Madeira

¾ cup Beef Stock (p. 213)
1 tablespoon lemon juice
Salt
Pepper
3 whole lemons, thinly sliced

Dredge veal in flour and sauté in butter over medium heat until brown. Remove veal from pan and set aside. Add wine, beef stock, lemon juice, salt, and pepper to pan juices. Stir and return the veal to the pan, placing a slice of lemon between each slice of veal. Cook for 5 minutes. This dish may be served with Almond Rice (p. 197). *Serves* 6

Veal Scaloppine Véronique
ROCHESTER ANDERSON

2 cups flour
Salt
Pepper
1 dozen slices of veal (about 5 ounces each), pounded into very thin 3-inch squares
2 tablespoons butter

1 teaspoon finely chopped shallots
2 tablespoons Marsala or sherry
⅔ cup Brown Sauce II (p. 233)
4 tablespoons green seedless grapes (canned grapes may be used)

Combine flour, salt, and pepper. Dredge veal slices with seasoned flour. Melt the butter in a skillet. Add the veal and brown on both sides until meat is fork-tender, about 10 minutes. Remove the veal to a serving dish and keep warm. Add the shallots to the skillet and simmer for 1 minute. Add the Marsala or sherry, brown sauce, and grapes. Bring to a boil and cook for 1 minute. Pour the sauce over the veal and serve. *Serves* 6

Veal Scaloppine Vin Rouge
NATHANIEL BURTON

4 tablespoons butter
6 4-ounce slices top round of veal
Salt
Pepper

2 cups flour
18 fresh mushrooms, sliced
3 green onions, chopped
2 cups red wine
Juice of 1 lemon

Melt butter in skillet. Rub the veal with salt and pepper and dredge with flour. Put veal in skillet and cook approximately 6 minutes. Remove from pan and add mushrooms and green onions. Cook gently until tender, then return veal to pan and add half the wine and the juice of 1 lemon. Simmer until liquid has reduced, approximately 6 minutes, and add the rest of the wine. (Pans are uncovered at all times.) *Serves* 6

Breaded Veal Chops
LEAH CHASE

½ teaspoon salt	½ cup whole or evaporated
¼ teaspoon pepper	milk
2 tablespoons flour	Breadcrumbs
4 veal chops	½ cup peanut oil
1 egg	

Combine salt, pepper, and flour. Dredge chops in flour mixture. Beat egg and milk together and dip the chops into the mixture. Roll in breadcrumbs, coating well. Refrigerate for 30 to 40 minutes. Heat the oil in a skillet and cook the chops slowly, browning on both sides. Drain on paper towels. *Serves* 4

Veal Lummie
CHARLES BAILEY

Salt	6 tablespoons butter
Pepper	¼ cup cooking oil
2 pounds veal, thinly sliced	½ pound fresh mushrooms,
2½ ounces lemon juice	sliced
1 cup milk	4 tablespoons Brown Sauce II
3 eggs, lightly beaten	(p. 233)
1 cup flour	6 tablespoons heavy cream
2 cups breadcrumbs	

Preheat oven to 375°. Salt and pepper veal to taste. Sprinkle lightly on both sides with lemon juice. Combine milk and eggs.

Dip veal first in flour, then in egg-and-milk mixture, then in breadcrumbs, pounding the crumbs well into the veal so that they will adhere. Melt butter and combine with oil in heavy ovenproof skillet. Place the veal in the pan and brown lightly on both sides. Place in oven for about 4 minutes. Remove veal from pan and keep warm. Sprinkle lemon juice over the mushrooms, add the brown sauce and heavy cream. Combine well, heat, and serve over the veal. *Serves* 6

Grillades with Tomato Sauce

RAYMOND THOMAS, SR.

Salt

Pepper

4 pounds veal, cut into 1½- to 2-inch strips

2½ cups flour

2 cups cooking oil

2 white onions, finely chopped

1 rib celery, finely chopped

2 green bell peppers, finely chopped

1 paw garlic, finely minced

1 10-ounce can tomatoes, crushed

6 tablespoons beef base (see Glossary, p. 315)

4 cups water

Salt and pepper the veal strips and dredge in flour, patting it in firmly. Reserve remaining flour. Heat cooking oil in saucepan until very hot and add the veal strips. Brown them on both sides, turning them quickly. Remove veal from pan and set aside. Add chopped vegetables to pan and stir in the remaining flour. Stir quickly to blend and add the tomatoes. Cook for 10 minutes, then add the beef base and water. Cover and simmer for 5 minutes. Return the veal to the pot and cook for 15 minutes longer.

This dish is traditionally served with grits for breakfast or brunch. *Serves 6 to 8*

Veal Kidneys Bordelaise
NATHANIEL BURTON

4 pounds veal kidneys,
washed and trimmed
1 bunch green onions, diced
1 dozen fresh mushrooms,
sliced
4 cloves garlic, minced

2 tablespoons chopped parsley
¼ pound butter
Salt
Pepper
3 cups Brown Gravy I (p. 233)
¾ cup red wine

Scald kidneys in boiling water and dice. Sauté green onions, mushrooms, garlic, and parsley with butter in skillet. Cook until tender. Add kidneys and cook 5 or 6 minutes, stirring constantly. Salt and pepper to taste. Coat another skillet lightly with butter and heat the brown gravy in it. When warm, add the kidney-vegetable mixture and cook for 10 minutes. Add wine and serve. *Serves 8*

Sweetbreads Montgomery
ROCHESTER ANDERSON

3 whole eggs
1 cup milk
6 8-ounce sweetbreads (preferably veal), sliced lengthwise into ¼-inch pieces
2 cups breadcrumbs
½ cup (1 stick) butter

½ cup flour
2 cups stock made from
sweetbread drippings
½ cup sliced fresh mushrooms
or truffles
Cooked asparagus tips

Beat eggs and milk together to make egg wash. Dip sweetbreads in wash and coat with breadcrumbs. Cook on an oiled grill for 5 minutes, turning so that pieces get evenly browned. Make a suprême sauce by sautéing the butter and flour gently for 5 minutes, adding the stock from the sweetbreads gradually. Simmer for 15 minutes. Just before serving, add mushrooms or truffles.

To serve, place the sweetbreads in the shape of a crown on a round platter, with the asparagus tips in the center. Serve the suprême sauce on the side. *Serves* 6

FOWL AND GAME

Chicken Financière

LARRY WILLIAMSON

2 roasting chickens, 2 to 2½
  pounds each, cut up
1 tablespoon butter
4 cups red gravy (see below)

1 cup fresh mushrooms, sliced
  (pieces and stems if canned)
6 ounces burgundy (or any
  other red wine)

Preheat oven to 350°. Bake chicken parts, except for livers, in oven for 40 minutes. Brown livers separately in a little butter, making sure they remain whole. Put baked chicken parts, red gravy, mushrooms, and wine in a large saucepan together with the chicken livers. Cook 20 minutes over very low heat.

Red Gravy

1 pound beef or veal, cut in two
2 quarts water

½ cup tomato purée
Salt and pepper

Boil meat for 10 minutes. Add tomato purée, salt, and pepper. Cook 10 minutes and strain. *Serves 6*

Poulet Majorca

ROCHESTER ANDERSON

4 tablespoons butter
Salt
1 2-pound chicken, trussed
4 tablespoons Calvados
1 tablespoon tomato paste
1 tablespoon glaze (see
  Glossary, p. 316)

3 tablespoons flour
2 cups Chicken Stock (p. 213)
½ cup dry white wine
1 tablespoon red currant jelly
Ground black pepper

Preheat oven to 375°. Heat the butter and salt in a heavy oven-proof skillet or casserole. When butter turns golden, put in the chicken, breast side down. Cover and brown slowly all over, using a wooden spoon inserted into the neck cavity to turn chicken. Do not pierce the flesh. When chicken has browned, heat Calvados, pour over chicken, and ignite. Let the flames subside, remove chicken from skillet, and set aside. Carve into serving pieces when cool.

Off heat, add tomato paste, glaze, and flour to the skillet, stirring well. When smooth, add chicken stock, dry white wine, jelly, and black pepper. Bring to a boil, remove from heat, and add chicken pieces. Place pan on the top shelf of oven and cook for 45 minutes, basting occasionally. *Serves 2 to 4*

Roast Long Island Duckling (Family Style)
CHARLES BAILEY

3 4-pound ducklings
Salt
Pepper
2 apples, quartered
1 teaspoon rosemary
2 leaves fresh thyme
3 ribs celery
2 bay leaves
1 onion, cut in sixths
3 cloves garlic

¾ cup flour
3 oranges, halved
4 cups Chicken Stock (p. 213)
1 cup vinegar
1 pound sugar
6 tablespoons Cointreau
4 tablespoons sherry
6 orange slices
Parsley

Preheat oven to 375°. Remove giblets and neck from ducklings and reserve. Salt and pepper ducklings inside and out. Stuff cavity with apples, rosemary, thyme, celery, bay leaves, onion, and garlic. Truss ducklings and place breast side up in a shallow roasting pan. Reduce oven temperature to 325° and cook for 1½ to 2 hours, or until golden brown. Remove ducklings from pan and set aside. When duckling has cooled, cut in half and remove breastbone and backbone. Add flour and orange halves to 1½ cups of drippings in pan. Place pan over medium heat on top of stove (or, preferably, leave in oven where heat is uniform) and stir frequently for 20 minutes or until liquid is reduced. Add chicken stock and cook for 30 to 40 minutes. Strain.

In a separate pan, stir vinegar into sugar until sugar dissolves. Cook until it becomes a light brown or caramel color. Add Cointreau and stir to blend. Mix into strained gravy and keep warm. Return duck to roasting pan. Sprinkle with sherry and heat in oven for 15 minutes. Remove from oven, place on serving dish, cover with sauce, and garnish with orange slices and parsley. *Serves* 6

Fried Chicken

AUSTIN LESLIE

1¼ cups peanut oil for frying
1 3- to 3 ½ pound fryer, cut up
Salt
Pepper
1 egg, lightly beaten

1 cup light cream or
  half-and-half
1 cup water
½ cup flour

Preheat oil in frying pan to about 350°. Wash chicken pieces under cold running water and pat dry. Sprinkle with salt and pepper. Make egg batter by combining egg, cream, water, salt, and pepper. Dip pieces of chicken first in egg batter to coat and then in flour. Add chicken pieces to skillet, meatiest parts first. Do not crowd. Turn to brown on all sides. If oil pops, reduce flame. Cook until meat is tender and skin crisp, about 10 to 12 minutes. *Serves* 6

Chicken New Orleans
SHERMAN CRAYTON

2 1½- to 2-pound chickens,
  cut in pieces
2 tablespoons vegetable oil
2 tablespoons flour
1 medium green bell pepper,
  cut in thin strips
1 medium onion, sliced
2 cups Chicken Stock (p. 213)

2 10-ounce cans tomatoes
6 oysters
1 dozen fresh shrimp
2 tablespoons parsley,
  chopped
4 fresh mushrooms, sliced
½ cup white wine
½ cup brandy

Sauté chicken pieces in oil until tender. Remove and set aside. Add flour to juices in pan and stir to make a roux. Add bell pepper and onion and sauté for 10 minutes, then add chicken stock and tomatoes. Cook another 5 minutes and return chicken pieces to pan. Add oysters, shrimp, parsley, and mushrooms and cook 15 minutes. Blend in wine and brandy, stir, and remove from heat. *Serves* 6

Note: Do not serve over rice.

Breast of Chicken Hawaiian
NATHANIEL BURTON

6 chicken breasts, whole,
  skin intact (about ½ pound
  each)
2 cups flour
Salt
Pepper
2 tablespoons butter

1 cup Chicken Stock (p. 213)
  or water
6 pineapple rings
6 slices white bread, toasted
1 cup Hollandaise Sauce III
  (p. 239, or use ready-made)

Dredge chicken breasts in flour, salt, and pepper. Melt butter in a skillet, brown the chicken breasts lightly, and cook until tender, about 7 minutes on each side. Remove from pan and add stock or water to pan drippings and stir to make gravy. For each serving, place a slice of pineapple on a piece of toast, add a spoonful of gravy and a chicken breast. Top with hollandaise sauce. *Serves* 6

Breast of Chicken Florentine
NATHANIEL BURTON

6 chicken breasts, whole, skin intact (about ½ pound each)
1 cup flour
Salt
Pepper
1 stick plus 2 tablespoons butter
2 10-ounce packages frozen spinach
4 cups Cream Sauce II (p. 235)
1 cup Cheddar cheese, grated

Preheat oven to 375°. Dredge chicken in flour mixed with salt and pepper. Melt butter in skillet and sauté chicken breasts until tender and brown, about 6-7 minutes on each side. Cook spinach according to package directions, drain, and combine with 2 cups of the cream sauce. In a saucepan blend the remaining 2 cups of the cream sauce with the grated cheese over low heat until well blended. Place the spinach and cream sauce mixture in the bottom of a 6 x 8 Pyrex baking dish, top with the cooked chicken breasts, and cover with the cheese sauce. Bake for 10 minutes or until cheese is brown and bubbling. *Serves* 6

Stewed Chicken with Brown Gravy
LEAH CHASE

1 5-pound stewing hen, cut up
Salt
Pepper
¼ cup vegetable oil
½ cup flour
2 cups onions, finely chopped
4 cups water
½ teaspoon fresh red pepper, crushed
1 teaspoon chopped parsley
2 cloves garlic, finely minced
½ teaspoon dried thyme

Season chicken pieces with salt and pepper. Heat oil in large skillet or deep pot and add chicken pieces. Cover tightly and cook for 30 minutes. Remove chicken and set aside. Add flour to drippings in pan and stir over low heat until flour is golden. Add onions and cook until they are translucent. Add water and gradually bring to boil. Return chicken to pot and add red pepper, parsley, garlic, and thyme. Cook slowly until chicken is tender, about 45 minutes. *Serves* 4

Boned Breast of Chicken on Ham
LOUIS EVANS

3 whole chicken breasts, skinned, boned and split, with wing tips removed but not wing bones
6 thin slices baked ham
3 eggs
Salt
Pepper
1 teaspoon water
Breadcrumbs
2¾ cups clarified butter (see Glossary, p. 315)
¼ cup glace de viande (See Glossary, p. 316) or meat extract
Lime slices
Sprigs of watercress

Preheat oven to 325°. Have butcher prepare breasts as directed above. Put breasts between 2 sheets of wax paper and pound thin with flat side of a cleaver. Trim the ham slices until they are the same size and shape as the flattened chicken breasts. Beat eggs lightly with salt, pepper, and water. Dip ham slices in egg mixture and press onto the halved chicken breasts. Dip ham-chicken pieces in egg mixture and roll in breadcrumbs, patting off the excess.

Using two large skillets, sauté the breaded chicken-ham pieces very carefully in 1 cup of the clarified butter until they are lightly browned on both sides. Transfer to a baking dish, reserving the butter and pan juices in the skillets.

Bake chicken breasts 10 to 20 minutes in oven, basting frequently. When done, remove from oven and keep warm while making sauce: Stir glace de viande or meat extract into the remaining 1¾ cups clarified butter and add to pan juices in skillets, dividing the amount equally. Stir well and pour over chicken. Garnish with lime slices and sprigs of watercress. *Serves* 6

Cornish Hen Mardi Gras
CORINNE DUNBAR'S

Salt	1 teaspoon Kitchen Bouquet
Pepper	2 tablespoons flour
8 Cornish hens, fresh, not frozen	1 tablespoon water
	½ cup Chablis
3 cups Chicken Stock (p. 213)	1 2-pound package wild rice,
3½ ounces pâté de foie gras	prepared according to
1 small can truffles, sliced	directions on package

Preheat oven to 350°. Salt and pepper hens. Place in pan and add 1 cup chicken stock. Brown in uncovered pan in oven for 25 minutes. Cover pan and steam for 20 to 25 minutes. While hens are cooking, make sauce. Heat 2 cups chicken stock in saucepan. Stir in pâté, sliced truffles, and Kitchen Bouquet. Combine flour and water and gradually add to sauce to thicken. Add Chablis just before serving. Pour sauce over hens and serve on a bed of wild rice. *Serves* 8

Coq au Vin

CHARLES BAILEY

Salt and pepper
1 3- to 4-pound capon (young rooster or hen), cut into serving pieces
Flour for dredging
¼ pound slab of pork fat, diced (or thick-sliced bacon)
1 medium onion, diced (white or yellow skin—do not use red-skinned onion)

1½ teaspoons flour
1 teaspoon tomato paste
4 cups Chicken Stock (p. 213)
¼ cup heavy cream
1 pound fresh mushrooms, sliced
1 or 2 bay leaves
¼ teaspoon thyme
1 clove garlic, minced
1½ cups burgundy or any other dry red wine

Preheat oven to 350°. Salt and pepper capon pieces. Dredge lightly with flour. Sauté diced pork until brown. Strain and remove pork to a side dish. Sauté the capon in the rendered pork fat in an ovenproof dish over low heat until capon is golden brown but not cooked through. Remove from pan and set aside. Add onion, flour, and tomato paste to fat in pan and cook roux slowly until golden. Stir in chicken stock and heavy cream. Return capon to pan, add mushrooms, the browned diced pork, bay leaves, thyme, garlic, and red wine. Cover and put in preheated oven for 35 to 40 minutes, or until capon is tender. Serve with rice or potato balls sautéed in butter (Parisienne Potatoes, p. 198) and a green vegetable. *Serves* 4

Stewed Chicken
AUSTIN LESLIE

1 5- to 6-pound stewing hen,
   cut into 12 pieces
Salt
Pepper
2 cups peanut oil
1 rib celery, chopped
1 medium onion, chopped
4 sprigs parsley, chopped
2 cups flour
1 gallon Chicken Stock (p. 213)
   or water

Season hen with salt and pepper. Heat oil in Dutch oven or heavy skillet and brown chicken pieces on all sides. Remove and set aside. Add celery, onion, and parsley to pot containing chicken drippings. Stir in flour and sauté gently for 15 to 20 minutes until browned. Add stock to pot and stir to prevent sticking. Return chicken pieces to pot, being sure that the stock covers the chicken. Cover pot and cook over medium heat for 1½ to 2 hours. *Serves 6*

Chicken Breasts Maitland
CORINNE DUNBAR'S

Salt
Pepper
8 whole chicken breasts,
   medium to large size, skin
   intact
2 cups Chicken Stock (p. 213)
¼ pound pork sausage meat
1 small onion, chopped
1 tablespoon flour
½ tablespoon water
1 teaspoon Kitchen Bouquet
¼ pound pecans, chopped
2 tablespoons sherry

Preheat oven to 350°. Salt and pepper chicken breasts to taste. Brown chicken breasts in uncovered pan in oven for 15 minutes in one cup of chicken stock. Cover pan and steam about 25 minutes more. To make sauce: Cook sausage until brown and remove from pan. Brown onion well in sausage fat. In blender, combine remaining chicken stock, onions, and sausage. Strain and pour in saucepan. In separate bowl, make paste of flour and water. Stir flour paste and Kitchen Bouquet into strained sauce. Cook until thick. Add pecans. Add sherry at the last minute. Pour over chicken breasts. *Serves* 8

Chicken and Dumplings

NATHANIEL BURTON

1 5- to 6-pound hen, cut in serving pieces
2 ribs celery, chopped
1 green bell pepper, chopped
1 medium-size onion, chopped

1 gallon water
½ pound butter
1 cup flour
1 #303 can peas (10 ounces)

Combine hen, celery, green pepper, onion, and water in a large pot. Bring to a boil. Reduce heat and simmer until tender (approximately 1 hour). Remove hen from pot, reserving the stock, and make sauce as follows: Blend butter and flour to make a roux. Add 2 cups of the stock to the roux; stir gently and cook over low heat until thickened. Reserve remaining chicken stock to cook dumplings.

Dumplings
2 cups flour
1½ teaspoons baking powder
¼ cup chicken fat

1 teaspoon white pepper
1 teaspoon salt
1 cup milk

Mix all ingredients together to make a dough. Roll out to ¼-inch thickness. Cut dough into squares or rectangles 1 to 2 inches wide. Drop dumplings into boiling chicken stock and cook about 10 minutes, or until done. Combine with chicken, peas, and sauce. *Serves* 8

Chicken Bonne Femme
RAYMOND THOMAS, SR.

4 chicken breasts, skinned
  and boned
Salt
Pepper
½ cup olive oil

4 potatoes, peeled and sliced
  into very thin rounds
½ pound ham, diced
2 cloves garlic, finely minced

Season chicken breasts with salt and pepper. Heat olive oil in skillet and sauté chicken lightly until brown. Remove from pan and set aside. Add potatoes, ham, and garlic to oil in pan and sauté until soft. Return chicken to pan and blend gently with other ingredients. Cook over low heat for 7 minutes and serve. *Serves 4 to 6*

Chicken Livers St. Pierre
RAYMOND THOMAS, SR.

1 pound chicken livers
Salt
Pepper
1 stick butter

1 can (16 ounces) green lima
  beans, drained
2 red bell peppers, diced
2 green bell peppers, diced

Season chicken livers with salt and pepper. Sauté lightly in butter, add the lima beans and the diced peppers. Simmer until done, approximately 12 to 15 minutes. *Serves 2*

Chicken Clemenceau

MALCOM ROSS

1 white potato, medium-size,
  diced
Oil for frying
2 1½- to 2-pound chickens,
  cut into serving pieces

1¾ cups butter
8 ounces fresh mushrooms,
  sliced
1½ tablespoons garlic, minced

Preheat oven to 350°. Diced potato must be cooked before hand. Deep-fry potato pieces for 4 to 5 minutes, or until they float to the top of the fryer. They should not be completely done at this stage.

Place chicken pieces in baking pan with 2 ounces butter and cook uncovered for 15 minutes. Remove from oven and place in saucepan along with mushrooms, fried potato pieces, and butter. Sauté for 5 minutes. Add garlic and serve. *Serves 6 to 8*

Turkey à la King

LARRY WILLIAMSON

2 cups Cream Sauce II
  (p. 235)
1½ pounds cooked turkey,
  cubed
1 green bell pepper, chopped
  and boiled until soft

1 small can pimentos
  (4 ounces), chopped
6 egg yolks
Salt
Pepper
6 tablespoons sherry

Combine all ingredients and stir over low heat for 10 minutes. Serve over toast. *Serves 6*

Heavenly Quail
ROCHESTER ANDERSON

4 quail
½ cup vegetable oil
4 tablespoons flour
Salt
Pepper
¼ cup butter

1 dozen large fresh mush-
    rooms, sliced
½ cup Sauterne or dry white
    wine
Hot buttered toast

Rub the skins of the quail generously with a small amount of the vegetable oil. Coat the quail with flour by shaking in a paper bag with flour, salt and pepper to taste. Heat the remaining oil in a heavy skillet or Dutch oven and brown the quail well on all sides. Transfer to a plate and keep warm. Drain all the oil from the skillet and melt the butter. Return the quail to the skillet together with the mushrooms and wine. Cover and cook over low heat for about 25 minutes or until tender. Serve the quail on thick slices of hot buttered toast and spoon some of the mushroom mixture over them. *Serves* 2

Quail with Wild Rice
ROCHESTER ANDERSON

¼ cup butter
1 cup fresh mushrooms,
    thinly sliced
¼ cup scallions, finely
    chopped
4 quail

1 cup Marsala
2 tablespoons lemon juice
Salt
Pepper
1 package wild rice, cooked
    according to directions

Preheat oven to 375°. Melt butter in skillet and lightly sauté mushrooms and scallions. Place the quail in a shallow baking pan and spoon the scallion-mushroom mixture around each one. Pour the butter remaining in the skillet over the birds and bake for about 30 minutes or until tender, basting frequently with the combined Marsala, lemon juice, salt, and pepper. To serve, arrange quail on a heated platter and pour the mushroom mixture over them. Serve cooked wild rice separately. *Serves* 2

Stewed Rabbit, Creole Style
NATHANIEL BURTON

2 young rabbits, cut up	3 cloves garlic, peeled and
Salt	crushed
Pepper	2 tablespoons parsley, finely
2 cups flour	chopped
¾ cup shortening	2 bay leaves
2 ribs celery, diced	1 #2½ can (2 pounds) toma-
1 medium onion, diced	toes, chopped (do not
1 green bell pepper, diced	substitute fresh tomatoes)

Preheat oven to 350°. Season rabbits with salt and pepper. Dredge with flour. Melt shortening in a heavy ovenproof skillet and sauté rabbit pieces until brown. Remove from skillet and set aside. Add celery, onion, and green pepper to juices in skillet and sauté until tender. Add the garlic, parsley, bay leaves, tomatoes, and rabbit pieces to skillet. Cover and cook in oven for 30 minutes. *Serves* 6 *to* 8

Venison Churchill

ROCHESTER ANDERSON

1 10-pound venison roast

Marinade
3 cups red wine
1 onion, chopped
½ rib celery, chopped
1 green bell pepper, finely
　chopped

4 bay leaves
1 tablespoon thyme
1 clove garlic, peeled and
　mashed
2 cups olive oil

Combine all the ingredients for the marinade. Place venison into large crock, pour in the marinade, and let the venison marinate overnight.

Preheat oven to 350°. Remove the venison from the marinade and place in roasting pan. Roast for 2 hours (allowing 12 minutes per pound of meat), basting with reserved marinade every 15 minutes. Meanwhile, make sauce.

Sauce
1 carrot, diced
1 medium onion, diced
¼ cup cooking oil
2 tablespoons bouquet garni
　(see Glossary, p. 315)
3 cups venison trimmings (fat
　drippings)

1 cup dry white wine
1½ cups wine vinegar
Salt
Pepper
3 tablespoons red currant jelly
2 tablespoons heavy cream

Heat vegetables slowly in oil. Add bouquet garni and venison trimmings and brown slightly. Drain off oil and pour in white wine and vinegar. Reduce almost completely and simmer for 1 hour. Add salt and pepper. Remove from heat, strain, and stir in jelly. When it is dissolved, add the cream and mix well. Keep hot until serving time.

Water-Chestnut Purée

4 pounds water chestnuts, cooked	Salt
	Pepper
¼ pound clarified butter (see Glossary, p. 315)	2 cups whipping cream

Preheat oven to 300°. Purée the water chestnuts in a blender or food mill and add the clarified butter, salt, and pepper. Put into small baking pan and bake for 30 minutes. Remove from oven and let cool. Stir in whipping cream just before serving.

Pears Cooked in Wine

10 fresh pears, peeled and cut in halves	4 cups sugar
	1 pound butter
4 cups water	2 cups red wine

Cook pears in water and sugar until firm but not mushy. Melt butter in skillet, add pears, and brown lightly. Add red wine and let finish cooking.

To serve

The meat should be carved in the kitchen and set on a platter with the chestnut purée and the pears in the center and the sauce as optional on the side. *Serves* 20

VEGETABLES

Rice Pilaf

CHARLES BAILEY

1 bay leaf
2 pinches fresh rosemary
   leaves
½ white onion, diced
¼ stick butter

4 ounces cooking oil
1 cup uncooked rice, washed
   and drained
4 cups Beef Stock (p. 213)
¼ cup raisins

Preheat oven to 375°. Sauté bay leaf, rosemary, and onion in melted butter and oil in an ovenproof casserole or Dutch oven. Cook for 3 to 4 minutes. Stir in rice and beef stock. Bake covered in oven until liquid is absorbed by the rice. Remove from oven. Stir in raisins and serve with Scampi Conti (p. 147). *Serves* 4

Almond Rice

NATHANIEL BURTON

1 stick butter
4 cups cooked rice
1 cup green peas

½ cup slivered almonds,
   toasted
Salt and white pepper

Melt butter in a saucepan and add the rice. Stir to coat rice with butter and cook for 5 minutes. Add peas and almonds. Stir. Season to taste with salt and white pepper. *Serves* 6

Potato Salad

AUSTIN LESLIE

1 pound Idaho potatoes
3 hard-boiled eggs
1 rib celery
4 sprigs parsley, chopped
½ cup Mayonnaise (p. 244, or
   ready-made)

2 tablespoons prepared yellow
   mustard
1 onion, diced
¼ cup cooking oil
Salt and pepper to taste

Peel and dice potatoes and boil until tender, approximately a half hour. Cool potatoes for a half to one hour. Chop eggs, celery, and parsley. Place potatoes in mixing bowl. Add eggs and seasonings. Stir in mayonnaise and mustard, onion, oil, salt, and pepper, Mix all ingredients until well blended. *Serves* 4

Kirkland's Homemade Potato Salad
CHARLES KIRKLAND

2½ pounds Idaho potatoes

3 green onions, finely chopped

1 cup Mayonnaise (p. 244, or ready-made)

¼ cup prepared yellow mustard

3 hard-boiled eggs

1 tablespoon parsley, chopped

3 tablespoons pimento, finely chopped

Salt and pepper to taste

Boil potatoes until the skin breaks. Peel and chop in large sections. Set aside. In a bowl mix remaining ingredients; then add potatoes, folding carefully so as not to mash them. Add salt and pepper to taste. *Serves* 6

Parisienne Potatoes
NATHANIEL BURTON

2 large Idaho potatoes

2 cups water

½ stick butter

1 teaspoon parsley, finely chopped

Salt to taste

Peel potatoes and, using a "Parisienne" scoop, form small potato balls. Place them in a saucepan and cover with water. Boil for 10 minutes. Melt butter in a skillet, add drained potato balls, and sauté for 8 minutes. Add parsley and salt to taste. *Serves* 2

Yams
AUSTIN LESLIE

1 pound yams (sweet potatoes)
Juice of 3 lemons (½ cup)
¾ cup sugar

Preheat oven to 350°. Wash yams and place in baking pan. Bake for 1 hour. After the first 15 minutes, puncture the yams once on top and bottom. After 1 hour of baking, take the yams out of the oven and peel while hot. Cut into 1½-inch cubes. Place in Pyrex baking dish and sprinkle with lemon juice and sugar. Return to oven for 30 minutes and serve. *Serves* 6

Stuffed Mirlitons I
CORINNE DUNBAR'S

4 mirlitons
¼ pound (1 stick) butter
½ pound ham, finely chopped
1 pound shrimp, boiled and
  ground
1 small onion, minced
2 cloves garlic, minced
2 sprigs thyme
2 bay leaves
1 tablespoon chopped parsley
½ loaf stale French bread
Salt
Pepper
Breadcrumbs
Pimento strips
Parsley sprigs

Preheat oven to 375°. Wash mirlitons well and parboil until tender (at least 1 hour for whole mirlitons). Halve, scoop out pulp, and save shells. Mash pulp and place in skillet with melted butter. Add ham, shrimp, onion, garlic, and seasonings and simmer for 20 minutes. Soak French bread in water and squeeze dry. Add to mixture, with salt and pepper to taste. Cook 10 minutes over low heat, stirring constantly. Fill mirliton shells with stuffing, sprinkle with breadcrumbs, and dot with butter. Place on baking sheet and put in oven until heated through. Garnish with pimento and parsley. *Serves* 8

Stuffed Mirlitons II
LEAH CHASE

3 mirlitons
1 tablespoon butter
½ pound shrimp, chopped
½ pound ground ham
1 onion, chopped
1 clove garlic, chopped

¼ teaspoon chopped parsley
¼ teaspoon minced fresh
  thyme
Salt
Pepper
¾ cup breadcrumbs

Preheat oven to 350°. Cut the mirlitons in half and remove seeds. Put into salted water and boil until tender, about 35 to 40 minutes. Remove from water and cool. Carefully scoop out the pulp and mash, leaving the shell in good condition for stuffing. Melt butter in pot, add shrimp, ham, onion, and garlic and cook until onions become transparent. Add the mashed mirliton pulp, parsley, thyme, and salt and pepper to taste. Cook 10 minutes and add the breadcrumbs, mixing well. Fill mirliton shells, sprinkling the top of each with additional breadcrumbs and dotting with butter. Place on baking sheet and bake for 15 minutes or until tops are lightly browned. *Serves* 6

Stuffed Peppers

AUSTIN LESLIE

3 large green bell peppers
½ pound (2 sticks) margarine
1 medium onion, finely
  chopped
1 rib celery, finely chopped
4 sprigs parsley (stems and
  leaves), finely chopped
Pinch of thyme
½ pound ground beef

½ pound small, fresh shrimp,
  peeled and deveined
½ loaf stale French bread
3 eggs
Salt
Pepper
1 teaspoon garlic powder
½ cup breadcrumbs

Preheat oven to 350°. Split peppers in half horizontally, remove seeds and membranes, wash, and set aside. Melt margarine in a large skillet, add onion, celery, parsley, and thyme and sauté for 10 to 15 minutes until cooked. Add ground beef and shrimp. In a large bowl, dampen bread until moist, squeeze out excess water, and add eggs. Mix well and then stir in sautéed ingredients. Blend, then add salt, pepper, and garlic powder. Place stuffing in baking pan or Pyrex dish and put in oven for 1½ hours. When done, chill in refrigerator. Fill peppers with chilled mixture (skim off any fat that appears after chilling), top each pepper half with breadcrumbs, and place on baking sheet. Put under medium flame in broiler for 15 to 20 minutes until warm.
Serves 6

Stuffed Eggplant I
MALCOM ROSS

2 eggplants
3 cups water
¼ cup green onions (or fresh chives), finely chopped
1 tablespoon fresh parsley, chopped
1 pound fresh lump crabmeat

1 pound fresh shrimp, peeled and deveined
2 tablespoons butter
2 cups Cream Sauce II (p. 235)
2 tablespoons breadcrumbs
Salt and pepper to taste

Preheat oven to 450°. Cut eggplants vertically in quarters. Put in a baking pan and cook uncovered in three cups of water in oven for 30 minutes. Sauté onions, parsley, crabmeat, and shrimp in butter for 5 minutes. Remove from heat. Add cream sauce and stir until blended. Scoop out the meat of the eggplant and add it to the sauce. Warm for 3 minutes. Add breadcrumbs, salt, and pepper and mix well. Put stuffing into eggplant shells, top with breadcrumbs and a little butter. Put in oven for 5 minutes. (A little of the stuffing may spill from the shell, but the baking will hold it together.) *Serves* 4 *to* 6

Stuffed Eggplant II
NATHANIEL BURTON

4 large eggplants, cut in half
¼ pound (1 stick) butter
1 cup finely chopped onions
1 cup soft bread, soaked in milk (use stale French bread)

1 pound crabmeat
1 tablespoon salt
1 teaspoon white pepper
Breadcrumbs

Preheat oven to 400°. Boil eggplants in salted water for 6 to 8 minutes. Drain. Carefully scoop the pulp from the shells and chop it fine. Melt the butter in a skillet and sauté the onions until tender. Add the eggplant pulp and the soft bread, blend, and cook 5 minutes. Add crabmeat, salt, and pepper. Cook 5 more minutes and fill eggplant shells with mixture. Sprinkle tops with breadcrumbs and bake for 10 minutes. *Serves* 8

Stuffed Eggplant III
BON TON

6 medium eggplants	1 pound fresh, small shrimp,
4 green bell peppers, chopped	peeled and deveined
4 medium onions, chopped	1 pound white lump crabmeat
½ cup celery, chopped	½ cup parsley, chopped
3 cloves garlic, minced	½ cup breadcrumbs
1 stick butter	1 teaspoon paprika

Preheat oven to 350°. Boil eggplants for 8 to 10 minutes. Cut in half and dig out the pulp. Place pulp in bowl. Save eggplant shells. Sauté peppers, onion, celery, and garlic all together in butter until limp. Then add eggplant pulp and sauté until dry. Add shrimp. Cook for another 15 to 20 minutes. Put all of these ingredients in another bowl and fold in crabmeat and parsley. Cool. Add enough breadcrumbs to give mixture stuffing consistency and place in the eggplant shells. Sprinkle a few more breadcrumbs on top and then sprinkle with the paprika. Dot with butter and bake until brown (approximately 15 minutes). *Serves* 12

Stuffed Eggplant IV
HENRY CARR

2 tablespoons butter
1 white onion, chopped
1 green bell pepper, chopped
2 ribs celery, chopped
2 cloves garlic, minced
½ pound ham, diced

2 eggplants
1 cup cracker crumbs
¼ cup grated parmesan
½ pound fresh lump crabmeat
Salt
Pepper

Preheat oven to 350°. Melt butter in skillet and sauté onion, bell pepper, celery, garlic, and ham for 10 minutes. Cut the eggplants into quarters and boil for 30 minutes. Scoop out the pulp and blend it with the vegetable-ham mixture. Fold in the cracker crumbs, cheese (reserving a little for the tops of the eggplants), and crabmeat. Add salt and pepper to taste and fill eggplant shells with mixture. Sprinkle with reserved cheese and crumbs and bake until brown. *Serves* 8

Stuffed Eggplant with Oysters
NATHANIEL BURTON

3 large eggplants
1 medium-size onion, chopped
2 ounces butter
2 dozen oysters

Salt and pepper
1 cup Italian Breadcrumbs
   (p. 267)

Preheat oven to 400°. Cut eggplant in half. Cover with water and boil 5 to 8 minutes, or just until tender. Remove from fire. Scoop out eggplant pulp and save shells. Sauté onion in butter until tender. Brown the oysters on top of open grill (or in frying pan) and add to onion. Chop the eggplant pulp and season with salt and pepper. Add ½ cup of the breadcrumbs, mix thoroughly, and fill shells. Sprinkle with remaining breadcrumbs. Bake in oven for 15 minutes. *Serves* 6

French-Fried Eggplant

LARRY WILLIAMSON

4 medium eggplants	2 cups Egg Wash (p. 107)
4 cups flour, seasoned with	3 cups breadcrumbs
salt and pepper	Fat for frying (vegetable oil)

Peel eggplants and cut lengthwise into 8 pieces. Dip eggplant sections in flour, then in egg wash, and roll in breadcrumbs. Heat fat in deep fryer to 360° and fry eggplant for 10 minutes. *Serves* 8

Creamed Spinach

HENRY CARR

3 pounds fresh spinach	1½ cups light cream
1½ cups water	Nutmeg
4 tablespoons unsalted butter	Salt
½ cup all-purpose flour	Black pepper

Wash the spinach leaves in cold running water, then cook in 1½ cups boiling salted water for 45 minutes, or until cooked down. Drain and squeeze to remove as much of the moisture as possible; chop fine. Heat the butter and add the flour to make a roux, stirring constantly with a wooden spoon to avoid scorching. Cook for about 10 minutes, add the cream, a dash of nutmeg, and the salt and pepper. Bring to a boil and simmer a few minutes. Pour into blender and blend at fast speed for 15 seconds. *Serves* 4

French-Style String Beans
LEAH CHASE

8 ounces (2 sticks) margarine
1 pound smoked ham, cut
   into 6 pieces
2 pounds fresh green beans,
   or 2 pounds frozen in bags
2 medium onions, finely
   chopped

3 medium potatoes, peeled
   and cut into quarters
Salt
Pepper

Melt margarine in a 4-quart pot. Add ham, stir, and cook for about 5 minutes over low heat. Add beans and onions, cover tightly, and cook for half an hour over medium heat. Add potatoes, salt, and pepper to taste. Cook until beans and potatoes are tender. *Serves* 6

Fried Artichoke Hearts
NATHANIEL BURTON

6 tablespoons grated
   parmesan
1 cup Italian Breadcrumbs
   (p. 267)

1 #303 can artichoke hearts
1 cup flour
Egg Wash (p. 107)
Fat for frying

Combine the cheese and breadcrumbs. Roll the artichoke hearts in flour, dip in egg wash, and roll in the cheese-and-breadcrumb mixture. Heat fat in deep fryer to 325° and fry artichokes for 3 or 4 minutes. *Serves* 4

Stuffed Cabbage
NATHANIEL BURTON

1 large cabbage
¼ pound (1 stick) butter
1 onion, diced
1 pound ground beef

2 cups cooked rice
1 tablespoon salt
1 teaspoon white pepper
½ cup Beef Stock (p. 213)

Preheat oven to 375°. Remove large outer leaves from cabbage and scald in hot, salted water. Drain and let cool. Melt butter in skillet and cook onion until tender, then add ground meat and cook 10 minutes. Add rice, salt, and pepper and stir well to combine. Place stuffing in cabbage leaves, roll up, and secure with toothpicks. Place in a baking pan, sprinkle with beef stock, and bake for 15 minutes. *Serves* 6

Scalloped Turnips with Peas
LEAH CHASE

3 cups turnips, cooked and
   mashed
1 cup green peas
¼ pound (1 stick) butter
¼ cup flour

2 cups milk
1 teaspoon salt
½ teaspoon white pepper
½ cup breadcrumbs
½ cup grated Romano cheese

Preheat oven to 375°. Put turnips and peas in casserole. Melt butter in saucepan and stir in flour. Add milk, stirring constantly until mixture thickens. Add salt and pepper. Pour over vegetables in casserole. Sprinkle with breadcrumbs and cheese and bake for 25 minutes. *Serves* 6

Stewed Okra with Ham

LEAH CHASE

3 pounds fresh okra
¼ cup cooking oil
1 pound smoked ham, cubed
1 cup chopped onions

1 #2 can whole tomatoes
Salt
Pepper

Wash okra and remove tops. Cut in pieces about 1 inch thick. Heat oil and sauté the ham until light brown. Add onions, okra, and tomatoes. Add salt and pepper to taste. Cook over low heat until okra is tender, about 15 minutes. *Serves* 6

Mustard Greens

AUSTIN LESLIE

4 bunches mustard greens
   (about 4 pounds)
1 pound pickled rib tips,
   chopped (see Glossary,
   p. 317)
1 cup water

1 onion, diced
1 rib celery, finely chopped
1 clove garlic, finely chopped
4 sprigs parsley, finely chopped
Salt
Pepper

Wash and clean greens and pull leaves off stems. Put meat in bottom of pot first with the cup of water; add onion, celery, garlic, and parsley and fill pot with greens. Cover. Cook over medium heat for 2 hours, stirring every 15 minutes. When done, add salt and pepper to taste. This recipe may also be used to prepare collards, turnips, cabbage, or string beans. *Serves* 4 *to* 6

French-Fried Onion Rings
LARRY WILLIAMSON

4 medium white onions
1 cup breadcrumbs
1 cup corn flour (See Glossary, p. 315)
2 cups Egg Wash (p. 107)
2 cups flour
Oil for deep-frying

Cut onions into ½-inch slices. Push out centers, then separate outer layers of onions. Combine breadcrumbs and corn flour. Dip onion rings in egg wash, then in flour, and then in the breadcrumbs-and-corn-flour mixture. Repeat, following same sequence, until the onion rings are used up. Deep-fry at 360° for 4 minutes. *Serves 4*

French-Fried Tomatoes
LARRY WILLIAMSON

4 medium ripe tomatoes, peeled and sliced (½ inch thick)
2 cups flour
1 cup Egg Wash (p. 107)
1 cup breadcrumbs
Salt and pepper to taste
Oil for deep-frying

Remove skin from tomatoes by dipping in boiling water or hot oil for 2 minutes, then carefully remove skin with a cloth or with paper towels. After skins are removed, slice tomatoes. Dip tomatoes in flour to cover, then dip in egg wash, then in breadcrumbs. Add salt and pepper to taste. Deep-fry at 360° for 4 minutes. *Serves 4*

STOCKS, SOUPS, AND GUMBOS

Beef Stock
NATHANIEL BURTON

5 pounds beef bones (shin
   bones preferred)
1 medium onion
2 fresh carrots

2 ribs celery
1 fresh bay leaf
½ teaspoon thyme
6 quarts water

Preheat oven to 450°. Split bones and roast in oven. When bones are thoroughly browned, place in large stockpot. Cut onions and carrots in half and put in roasting pan with celery pieces. Braise in oven, add to stockpot along with bay leaf and thyme. Pour in 6 quarts of water. Cook slowly for at least 8 hours. *Makes approximately 2 quarts of stock*

Chicken Stock
NATHANIEL BURTON

1 whole 5- to 6-pound hen
1 medium onion, chopped
3 ribs celery, chopped

2 carrots, chopped
2 fresh bay leaves
5 quarts water

Put all ingredients in a 2-gallon pot. Simmer slowly until hen is tender, approximately 2½ hours. Let stock cool with hen in it. Remove hen and strain. *Stock will keep one week refrigerated. Makes 4 quarts*

Shrimp or Shellfish Stock
NATHANIEL BURTON

10 pounds fresh whole
   shrimp, shells intact
1 onion, chopped

2 ribs celery, chopped
4 fresh bay leaves
4 quarts water

Place all ingredients in a 2-gallon pot. Boil for 5 minutes. Let shrimp cool in water. Strain. *Makes 1¼ gallons*

Fish Stock
NATHANIEL BURTON

5 pounds fish bones
2 medium onions, chopped
3 ribs celery, chopped

2 carrots, chopped
4 fresh bay leaves
4 quarts water

Put all ingredients in 2-gallon pot. Simmer for 30 minutes. Cool and strain. Stock will keep 1 week refrigerated. *Makes 1 gallon*

Vegetable Soup
NATHANIEL BURTON

1 gallon cold water
2 pounds short ribs cut in
   bite-size pieces
1 bay leaf
1 cup chopped onion
6 carrots, peeled and diced
4 whole ripe tomatoes

2 cups potatoes, peeled and
   diced
1 cup fresh lima beans
2 ears fresh corn cut from the
   cob
Salt and pepper to taste

In soup pot, put one gallon cold water. Add short ribs and bay leaf and cook over low heat for 1½ hours. Add all other ingredients except salt and pepper and let cook at least 1 hour longer. Salt and pepper to taste. *Serves 8*

Green Split-Pea Soup
NATHANIEL BURTON

2 ounces vegetable shortening
1 onion, peeled and diced
2 ribs celery, chopped
2 medium carrots, peeled and
   chopped
1 gallon cold water

1 pound green split peas
1 ham bone
2 bay leaves
3 tablespoons cornstarch
Salt and pepper to taste

Melt shortening and put in soup pot with onion, celery, and carrots. Sauté until tender, about 5 minutes. Add the water, split peas, ham bone, and bay leaves. Simmer about 1½ hours. Remove from heat, add cornstarch and seasonings, and strain through fine chinois cap (see Glossary, p. 315). *Serves* 8

Cream of Mushroom Soup
NATHANIEL BURTON

½ pound (2 sticks) butter
1 pound fresh mushrooms,
   sliced
½ cup flour
3 quarts Chicken Stock,
   heated (p. 213)

4 cups half-and-half (or light
   cream), heated
Salt and pepper to taste

Melt butter in soup pot and add mushrooms. Cook until soft, add flour, and blend into a smooth roux. Cook slowly for about 5 minutes, add chicken stock, and let simmer about 15 minutes. Blend in half-and-half, season, and serve. *Serves* 8

Cream of Broccoli Soup
LOUIS EVANS

2 bunches fresh broccoli,
   about 2 pounds
2 quarts Chicken Stock (p. 213)
2 ribs celery
1 small white onion, peeled
½ bunch green onions,
   chopped

4 tablespoons butter
2 tablespoons flour
Salt to taste
Pepper to taste
1 bay leaf
Thyme to taste
2 cups half-and-half

Separate the broccoli into stems and flowerets and peel the stems carefully. Gently boil half of the broccoli in the chicken stock for about 30 minutes, or until tender. In another pan, sauté the celery, onion, and green onions in butter. Add the flour and cook for 5 minutes. Strain the liquid from the broccoli-stock mixture into the sautéed celery and onions. Chop the remaining broccoli into bite-size pieces, add to stock, and simmer for 10 minutes. Add salt, pepper, bay leaf, and thyme. Heat half-and-half, blend into soup, and serve. *Serves* 6

Red Bean Soup
CORINNE DUNBAR'S

1 small onion, peeled and
   chopped
¼ stick (1 ounce) butter
1 quart water
½ pound red kidney beans
2 cloves garlic, peeled and
   chopped
2 ribs celery, chopped
2 bay leaves

2 sprigs fresh thyme, or 1
   teaspoon dried thyme
1 teaspoon Worcestershire sauce
½ pound ham, finely ground
Salt
Pepper
6 tablespoons claret
2 hard-boiled eggs, riced
Lemon slices

Brown onion in butter, add water and all remaining ingredients except the last six. (You may place thyme and bay leaf in a muslin bag for simmering.) Simmer for about 2 hours, then strain mixture by mashing through a coarse sieve with a large spoon. Add ham and salt and pepper to taste. Place 1 tablespoon claret in the bottom of each serving bowl. Pour soup into bowl and garnish with a little riced egg and a lemon slice. *Serves* 6

Crab Bisque

NATHANIEL BURTON

1 small onion, peeled and chopped
¼ stick (1 ounce) butter
1 quart water
½ pound red kidney beans
2 cloves garlic, peeled and chopped
2 ribs celery, chopped
2 bay leaves
2 sprigs fresh thyme, or 1 teaspoon dried thyme
1 teaspoon Worcestershire sauce
½ pound ham, finely ground
Salt
Pepper
6 tablespoons claret
2 hard-boiled eggs, riced
Lemon slices

Melt butter in soup pot. Add crabs and cook until all water is out of them. Stir in celery and onion and cook until tender, about 5 minutes. Do not brown. Add flour, blend into a smooth roux, and cook for about 5 minutes. Add chicken stock, stir, and bring to a boil. Add bay leaf and simmer at least 30 minutes. Heat half-and-half and blend into soup. Strain through fine chinois cap (see Glossary, p. 315) and season with salt and pepper. Add crabmeat and serve. *Serves* 8

Crayfish Bisque
CORINNE DUNBAR'S

2 pounds crayfish. Separate heads from tails, clean heads

1 pound shrimp (with heads, in shell)

3 quarts water

2 medium onions, 1½ onions in soup, ½ an onion in stuffing

1 clove garlic, use ¼ clove in stuffing

3 ribs celery, 2 ribs in soup, 1 in stuffing

6 sprigs fresh thyme, 4 in soup, 2 in stuffing

2 bay leaves (in soup only)

2 cloves (optional—in soup only)

Salt

Pepper

Cayenne

4 ounces tomato paste, 3 in soup, 1 in stuffing

½ cup flour and ¼ cup water, combined

1 teaspoon Kitchen Bouquet

2 tablespoons shortening

½ loaf French bread, moistened and in pieces

To make soup

Soak crayfish in strong salt water for 1 hour. Drain, rinse, and drain again. Boil shrimp in 1 quart lightly salted water for a few minutes. Remove and reserve water. Peel and chop shrimp finely and reserve for stuffing. Save the shrimp heads and put them in the reserved shrimp water. Add 2 quarts of water to the shrimp water and add the crayfish and soup vegetables, seasonings, and tomato paste listed above. Boil 30 to 40 minutes. Remove crayfish and set aside. Strain broth. Make a paste of the combined ½ cup flour and ¼ cup water, add the Kitchen Bouquet. Add slowly to broth and simmer 2 hours, stirring frequently.

To make stuffing

Peel crayfish tails (save heads) and chop meat finely. Combine with chopped shrimp. Sauté shrimp and crayfish in shortening, add vegetables, seasonings, and tomato paste, and simmer 30 minutes. Add the pieces of French bread and simmer 20 minutes longer, stirring constantly. When mixture is cool, stuff crayfish heads. (The heads may be browned in the oven before serving.) Pour the soup into individual soup bowls and garnish each with 3 or 4 of the stuffed crayfish heads. *Serves* 10

Artichoke Bisque
SHERMAN CRAYTON

½ stick butter
3 tablespoons flour
1 quart water
½ rib celery, finely chopped
2 medium white onions,
   peeled and finely chopped
2 bay leaves

1 clove garlic, chopped
1 #2 can artichoke hearts,
   undrained
Salt
Pepper
½ cup white wine

Melt butter, add flour, and cook for about 5 minutes. *Do not brown.* Add water and stir. Add celery, onions, bay leaves, and garlic and boil gently for about half an hour. Mash the hearts of artichoke and add to soup along with the artichoke water. Cook for another half hour, then stir in salt and pepper to taste. Add the wine and serve. *Serves* 4

Oyster and Artichoke Soup

LOUIS EVANS

2 quarts oysters
½ gallon water
½ bunch green onions (about
    ½ cup)
1 rib celery, chopped
¼ white onion, chopped
1 teaspoon thyme
½ teaspoon salt
2 bay leaves

Pepper
8 ounces butter
¼ cup flour
1 #303 can artichokes,
    undrained (8 to 10 arti-
    chokes per can)
1 tablespoon chicken base or 1
    chicken bouillon cube

Bring oysters to boil in water, skimming to remove scum. Sauté vegetables and seasonings in butter for 5 minutes. Add flour and cook for another 5 minutes. Pour oysters and stock over the sautéed mixture and add artichokes with their water. Add chicken base or bouillon cube and cook for another 10 to 15 minutes. *Serves 8 to 10*

Oyster Soup I

SHERMAN CRAYTON

1 bunch scallions, chopped
2 ounces butter or margarine
2 tablespoons flour
2 cups oyster water (water
    drained from oysters plus
    tap water to make 2 cups)

24 oysters
Salt and pepper
1 quart water
1 teaspoon fresh parsley,
    chopped

Sauté scallions in butter or margarine for 3 to 4 minutes, being careful not to let them brown. Add flour and cook another 5 minutes. Add oyster water and simmer for 15 minutes. Add water, oysters, salt, and pepper and cook in 1 quart water for 15 minutes. Sprinkle with parsley and serve. *Serves 6*

Oyster Soup II
NATHANIEL BURTON

1 quart fresh open oysters
2 quarts oyster water (add tap
   water to oyster liquid to make
   2 quarts)
1 bay leaf
1 stick butter
¼ bunch (½ cup) green
   onions, chopped

1 rib celery, chopped
¼ cup flour
Salt
Pepper
Dash Worcestershire sauce
3 teaspoons fresh parsley,
   chopped

Put oysters, oyster water, and bay leaf in pot and bring to boil. Skim. In a soup pot, melt butter, add onion and celery, and sauté at least 5 minutes. Add flour, blending to make a roux, and cook for about 5 minutes more. Stir in oysters and oyster water, blending until smooth. Let cook for about 20 minutes, then season to taste with salt, pepper, and Worcestershire sauce. Sprinkle with parsley before serving. *Serves* 8

Oyster Soup III
MALCOM ROSS

1½ sticks butter
¼ cup flour
½ cup green onions, chopped
1½ quarts oyster water

2 dozen oysters
Salt
Pepper

Make a roux with the butter and flour. Sauté gently 5 minutes, then add onions and oyster water. Stir and let simmer 20 minutes. Add oysters and simmer for 10 minutes more. Salt and pepper to taste. *Serves* 4

Turtle Soup I
CORINNE DUNBAR'S

2 pounds fresh turtle meat

4 quarts water

8 beef bouillon cubes

1 white onion, minced

1 clove garlic, minced

3 ribs celery, finely chopped

3 sprigs fresh thyme

3 bay leaves

4 whole cloves

½ lemon, sliced

Dash of Tabasco sauce

1 cup flour

¼ cup water

1 teaspoon Kitchen Bouquet

Salt

Pepper

Sherry

Lemon slices

Hard-boiled eggs, riced

Boil turtle meat slowly in water until tender (about 2 hours). Remove meat and chop in small pieces. Strain stock, dissolve bouillon cubes in it, and return meat to stock. Add onion, garlic, celery, thyme, bay leaves, cloves, lemon, and Tabasco. Make a paste of 1 cup of flour and ¼ cup water and slowly stir into soup to thicken. Simmer 2 to 3 hours. Add Kitchen Bouquet, salt, and pepper. Serve in soup bowls. Garnish each bowl with 2 teaspoons sherry, 1 lemon slice, and 2 teaspoons riced eggs. *Serves* 8

Turtle Soup II

LOUIS EVANS

2 pounds turtle meat
Salt
Pepper
3 tablespoons vegetable oil
3 tablespoons flour
2 large onions, chopped
2 ribs celery, chopped
1 green bell pepper, seeded
  and chopped
1 cup tomato sauce
1 cup water
½ lemon, sliced
4 bay leaves
8 cups water
1 sprig parsley, chopped
¼ cup sherry
1 tablespoon Worcestershire
  sauce
3 hard-boiled eggs, halved

Season turtle meat with salt and pepper and fry in oil until brown. Remove from pan and set aside. Add flour to oil and brown slowly until golden. Stir in onions, celery, and bell pepper and cook until tender, about 5 minutes. Return the turtle meat to mixture, add tomato sauce and 1 cup water, and cook for about 30 minutes. Add lemon, bay leaves, and 8 cups water and simmer for 1 hour or until soup has reached the desired thickness. Add parsley, sherry, and Worcestershire sauce and stir to blend. Serve in soup bowls with half a hard-boiled egg. *Serves 6 to 8*

Turtle Soup III
RAYMOND THOMAS, SR.

5 pounds turtle meat, cut into
  bite-size pieces
2 cups cooking oil
2 cups flour
2 cups sherry
6 white onions, finely
  chopped
2 bunches green onions,
  finely chopped
1 rib celery, finely chopped

5 lemons, finely chopped
6 bay leaves, crushed
1 whole paw of garlic
1 sprig fresh thyme
5 quarts water
1 10-ounce can whole
  tomatoes
1 10-ounce can tomato purée
Sherry

In a 2-gallon pot, fry turtle meat in the oil until dry. Remove
from pot. Add flour to make a roux in the same pot. Add sherry,
chopped vegetables, and seasonings, including lemons, to the
roux and cook for 3 minutes. Add 5 quarts of water, tomatoes,
and purée. Let simmer for 1 hour, add sherry and serve. Vary
quantity of sherry used to taste. *Serves* 12 *to* 15

Creole Turtle Soup I
NATHANIEL BURTON

1 cup butter
½ cup all-purpose flour
1 medium-size onion, chopped
1 rib celery, chopped
1 #303 can tomato purée
3 quarts Beef Stock (p. 213)
2 pounds green turtle meat,
  diced

1 bay leaf
1 teaspoon *each* oregano,
  thyme, sweet basil, marjoram,
  allspice, and whole cloves
2 lemons, halved
6 bard-boiled eggs, chopped
½ cup sherry

Melt ½ cup of butter in a soup pot. Add flour and make a brown roux. Add onion and celery. Cook until tender. Add purée and beef stock and stir until smooth. Bring to a boil and skim. Melt ½ cup butter in a heavy skillet and add turtle meat. Cook until dry (all moisture should be out of the meat). Tie seasonings in a piece of cheesecloth and place in the soup. Add lemons and let simmer at least 40 minutes. Remove bag of seasonings before serving. Garnish soup with eggs and serve with sherry. *Serves* 8

Creole Turtle Soup II

SHERMAN CRAYTON

½ pound turtle meat, cubed
1 cup cooking oil
3 tablespoons flour
2 green bell peppers, chopped
2 medium white onions,
　peeled and chopped
1 cup green onions, chopped
½ cup parsley, finely chopped
4 ribs celery, chopped
2 cloves garlic, peeled and
　minced

1 ounce thyme
8 cups water (2 quarts)
2 cups peeled, seeded tomatoes,
　crushed, or 1 10-ounce can
½ lemon, sliced
2 hard-boiled eggs, chopped
⅛ cup whole cloves, mashed
Salt
Pepper
2 bay leaves
¼ cup sherry

Sauté turtle meat in oil until brown, about 5 minutes. Remove from pan and set aside. Add flour to oil and brown to a roux texture. Add peppers, onions, green onions, parsley, celery, garlic, and thyme. Cook slowly for about 15 minutes, stirring continuously. Add water and tomatoes and simmer for 45 minutes to 1 hour. Add turtle meat, lemon, eggs, cloves, salt, pepper, and 2 bay leaves, and cook for 30 minutes longer. Stir in sherry just before serving. *Serves* 3 *to* 4

Crab Bouillon
CORINNE DUNBAR'S

1 pound shrimp (with heads,
  if possible, and in shell)
1 gallon water
1 small onion
1 clove garlic
2 ribs celery
1 bay leaf

2 sprigs fresh thyme
2 whole cloves
Salt
Pepper
½ cup flour
¼ cup water
1 pound white crabmeat

Boil whole shrimp in water with all vegetables and seasonings for 10 minutes. Drain and reserve stock. Peel and grind shrimp. Make paste of ½ cup flour and ¼ cup water and stir into stock to thicken. Add ground shrimp and crabmeat. *Serves* 12

Creole Gumbo I
RAYMOND THOMAS, SR.

¼ pound okra, cut up
½ cup oil
½ cup flour
½ pound shrimp (peeled and
  deveined)
3 hard-shell crabs (cut in half)
1 green bell pepper, finely
  chopped
1 white onion, finely chopped
1 bunch green onions, finely
  chopped

½ celery rib, finely chopped
2 cloves garlic, finely minced
1 bay leaf
1 sprig thyme
1 10-ounce can whole
  tomatoes
1 10-ounce can tomato purée
Salt and pepper to taste
1 quart water
½ pint oysters (optional)

In a pan, sauté okra in 1 teaspoon of oil for 7 to 8 minutes. In a 1-gallon pot, make roux with oil and flour, stir at least 5 minutes. Add seafood, vegetables, seasonings, tomatoes, and tomato purée to roux and sauté for 5 minutes. Add water, stir, then add okra and cook on low to medium flame for 1 hour. If you wish, add oysters just before serving. Do not store with oysters. *Serves* 6 *to* 8

Creole Gumbo II

HENRY CARR

4 hard-shell crabs
2 pounds whole fresh shrimp
  (with shells intact and
  heads as well, if possible)
2 gallons water (for shrimp
  stock)
1½ pounds okra
4 ounces butter
1 cup vegetable oil or olive oil
1 cup flour
1 large onion, chopped
1 large green bell pepper,
  chopped

3 ribs celery, chopped
¼ cup green onions, tips only,
  chopped
1 #2 can tomatoes
1 teaspoon filé powder
1 cup dried shrimp (see
  Glossary, p. 316), optional
Dash Tabasco sauce
Dash Worcestershire sauce
1 pound fresh lump crabmeat
Salt
Pepper

Remove shells and entrails and cut crabs into sections. Peel shrimp and put aside. Boil shells and heads in 2 gallons water to make stock. Allow water to stay at boiling point while preparing rest of recipe. In separate pan, sauté okra in butter until dry, being careful not to burn it. In 2¼-gallon pot, heat oil, add flour, and stir until golden brown. Add onion, green pepper, celery, and green onions and sauté until soft. Add hard-shell crabs and tomatoes and sauté for 3 minutes. Stir in filé powder and slowly pour in boiling stock. Add cooked okra, dried shrimp (if you wish), Tabasco, Worcestershire sauce, reserved raw shrimp, and lump crabmeat. Salt and pepper to taste. Lower heat and cook for 1 hour. Add shrimp 5 minutes before cooking time is completed. Add crabmeat 3 minutes before serving. *Serves* 8 *to* 10

Dooky's Creole Gumbo

LEAH CHASE

4 hard-shell crabs, cleaned*
½ pound Creole hot sausage (see Glossary, p. 316), cut in bite-size pieces
½ pound smoked sausage, cut in pieces
½ pound beef, cubed
½ pound smoked ham, cubed
½ cup peanut oil
4 tablespoons flour
1 cup chopped onions
3 quarts water
6 chicken wings, cut in half
1 pound shrimp, peeled and deveined
1 tablespoon paprika
1 tablespoon salt
1 tablespoon filé powder
2 dozen oysters, with their liquid
¼ cup (2 ounces) chopped parsley
3 cloves garlic, minced
1 teaspoon ground thyme

Put crabs, sausages, stew meat, and ham in a 5-quart pot over a medium flame. Cover and let cook in its own fat for 25 minutes. (It will produce enough, but stay with the pot.) Heat oil in skillet and add flour to make a roux, browning until golden. Add onions and cook over low heat until onions wilt. Pour the onion mixture over the ingredients in the large pot. Add water, chicken wings, shrimp, paprika, salt, and filé powder. Bring to a boil and cook for 30 minutes. Add the oysters, parsley, garlic, and thyme. Lower heat and cook for 10 minutes more before serving. *Serves 8 to 10*

* Remove shells, entrails, and legs. Cut crabs in half and use along with paws.

Okra Gumbo

NATHANIEL BURTON

2 pounds medium-size fresh shrimp (with shells)
1 gallon Chicken Stock (p. 213)
⅓ cup butter
3 pounds okra, sliced
1 large onion, finely chopped
1 green bell pepper, finely chopped
1 clove garlic, minced
2 tablespoons chopped parsley
1½ cups canned tomatoes (1 #2 can)

Peel and clean shrimp. Put shells in the chicken stock and boil at least 10 minutes. Strain and set aside. Melt the butter in a soup pot. Add the okra, onion, and green pepper and sauté until liquid has evaporated. Add garlic and chopped parsley and cook for about 2 minutes more, then add the strained chicken stock and the tomatoes. Stir thoroughly and add the shrimp. Cook over medium heat for about 30 minutes. Serve with rice. *Makes 10 servings*

Filé Gumbo

AUSTIN LESLIE

½ pound margarine
1 rib celery, chopped
4 sprigs parsley, finely chopped
1 onion, finely chopped
½ cup flour
1 gallon Shellfish Stock (p. 213)
½ pound smoked ham, diced
6 crabs, in shells
½ pound Creole hot sausage (see Glossary, p. 316), cut in bite-size pieces
½ pound smoked sausage, cut in bite-size pieces
½ pound shrimp, cleaned and shelled (reserve shells for stock)
Salt
Pepper
2 tablespoons filé powder

Place margarine at bottom of a large soup or seafood pot, add celery, parsley, and onion. Sauté and then simmer for 15 to 20 minutes over low heat. Add flour and stir constantly for 15 more minutes. Add stock and heat over medium flame for 20 minutes. Stir in ham, crabs, and sausages and cook for 30 minutes. Bring to a boil and keep stirring to avoid mixture sticking. When pot returns to boil, add shrimp, salt, pepper, and filé powder and allow to return to the boiling point again. Remove from heat and check seasoning, adding more if needed. *Serves* 10 *to* 12

SAUCES AND DRESSINGS

Brown Gravy or Brown Sauce I
NATHANIEL BURTON

3 tablespoons butter
3 tablespoons flour
8 cups Beef Stock (p. 213)

Melt butter, stir in flour, and make an evenly browned roux. Slowly add beef stock to brown roux. Stir and blend. Let boil a minute or two and then simmer at least 20 minutes. This sauce will be fairly thin but will thicken when heated for use in recipes. *Makes 8 cups*

Brown Gravy or Brown Sauce II
ROCHESTER ANDERSON

1 tablespoon vegetable shortening
1 tablespoon flour
3 cups instant stock: 3 cups water and 4 beef bouillon cubes

Melt shortening in a saucepan or skillet and add flour. Blend and cook over medium flame until brown (approximately 20 minutes). Add stock and simmer for 30 minutes more. *Makes 3 cups*

Brown Mushroom Sauce
NATHANIEL BURTON

4 ounces butter

½ pound fresh mushrooms,
   sliced

4 cups Brown Sauce I (p. 233)

2 cups red wine

Juice of ½ a lemon

Melt butter in saucepan; add mushrooms and sauté until brown. Add brown sauce and half of wine. Simmer until reduced to one quart liquid. Add remaining wine and lemon juice. *Makes 5 cups*

Cream Sauce I
ROCHESTER ANDERSON

3 tablespoons flour
3 tablespoons butter, melted
1½ cups milk

In saucepan, blend flour and butter and cook for 5 minutes on medium flame to make a white roux. Add milk and simmer for another 5 minutes, or until mixture thickens. Cool before serving. *Makes about 2 cups*

Cream Sauce II
MALCOM ROSS

2 quarts milk
1 cup flour
1 pound butter

Put milk in a pot and heat on medium flame. Mix flour and butter in a separate pot and heat on medium flame. When milk is hot, stir into the flour and butter mixture. Let mixture come to a boil and take off stove. *Makes 2 quarts cream sauce; use 5 ounces per serving*

White Sauce
NATHANIEL BURTON

1 quart milk
½ cup all-purpose flour
½ pound butter, melted
2 egg yolks, beaten

Pour milk in a saucepan and bring to boiling point. In another saucepan, combine flour and melted butter to make a white roux. Cook, but do not brown. Stir in the hot milk. Beat with whisk until smooth and thickened. Add egg yolks and remove from heat. *Makes 5 cups*

White Mushroom Sauce
NATHANIEL BURTON

2 ounces butter
2 green onions, cut fine
½ pound fresh mushrooms,
   sliced thin

1½ cups Sauterne
4 cups Cream Sauce I (p. 234)

Melt butter in saucepan. Add green onions and mushrooms. Sauté until tender. Add wine and cream sauce. Cook about 5 minutes. Use with fish, veal, or chicken. *Makes about 5 cups*

Mornay Sauce
NATHANIEL BURTON

½ pound swiss cheese, grated
2 ounces parmesan cheese, grated
1 tablespoon Worcestershire sauce
4 cups Cream Sauce I (p. 234)

Put all ingredients in cream sauce and heat slowly until cheese has melted. Serve with fish, veal, or chicken. *Makes about 4 cups*

Béchamel Sauce
CHARLES KIRKLAND

1 quart milk
4 ounces butter
¼ cup white onion, chopped
1 cup flour

Heat milk in a saucepan. In another heavy 2-quart saucepan, melt the butter and add onion. Cook for 5 minutes over a low flame. Blend in flour and cook 5 minutes more. Add the hot milk slowly to the butter-onion-flour mixture and cook for 10 minutes. Strain. *Makes 1 quart*

Basic Tomato Sauce
NATHANIEL BURTON

3 ounces olive oil
2 onions, finely chopped
2 ribs celery, finely chopped
4 ounces fresh sliced mushrooms (stems and caps)

6 cloves garlic, minced
1 pound fresh tomatoes,
   crushed
1 #303 can tomato paste
4 cups water

Heat oil in saucepot. Add onions and celery and brown. Add mushrooms and garlic. Sauté about 3 minutes. Add crushed tomatoes and tomato paste. Add water. Let cook at least 1 hour. Put in a covered jar, store in refrigerator, and use as needed. *Makes about 6 cups*

Grillades à la Creole Sauce
NATHANIEL BURTON

3 ounces olive oil
1 large onion, finely chopped
2 green bell peppers, finely
   chopped
4 cloves of garlic, minced
2 tablespoons chopped parsley

2 bay leaves
4 cups tomato purée
1 tablespoon sugar
Salt and pepper to taste

Pour oil in saucepan and heat. Add onion and green peppers; sauté until soft. Add garlic, parsley, and bay leaves, cook about two minutes and add tomato purée. Add sugar and salt and pepper to taste. *Makes 5 cups*

Creole Sauce
MALCOM ROSS

¼ pound (1 stick) butter
1 medium onion, chopped
1 green bell pepper, chopped
½ bunch celery, chopped
2 10-ounce cans tomatoes
2 10-ounce cans tomato purée

3 bay leaves
¼ ounce thyme
Salt and pepper to taste
1 tablespoon sugar
½ cup cornstarch
½ cup water

Melt butter in 2-quart saucepan. Add all ingredients except cornstarch and water. Cook over medium flame for 1 hour or until celery is tender. Mix cornstarch and water in a separate bowl until creamy. Stir into vegetable mixture and cook 20 minutes more. *Makes 8 cups*

Hollandaise Sauce I
HENRY CARR

½ pound (2 sticks) butter
4 egg yolks
1 ounce tarragon vinegar

4 drops Tabasco sauce
1 ounce lemon juice
1 tablespoon tap water

Let butter come to slow boil. Combine eggs, vinegar, and Tabasco in a mixing bowl and beat well. Add hot butter slowly, beating constantly until mixture thickens. Add lemon juice and water. *Makes 1½ cups*

Hollandaise Sauce II

MALCOM ROSS

1 dozen egg yolks
½ pound butter, melted
½ ounce wine vinegar
Salt to taste
Cayenne pepper to taste

1 cup cold water
2 pounds butter (melted
  and cooled to room
  temperature)

Put egg yolks in top of a large double boiler with ½ pound of melted butter, vinegar, salt, and cayenne. Add small amount of water to bottom of double boiler (enough to cook the eggs after mixture reaches a boil). Place pot over a high flame.

Beat with a wire whip until eggs are almost scrambled. Take off fire and add 1 cup of cold water. Continue to whip. Add small amounts of melted butter as you whip until all the butter has been used. Keep sauce at room temperature. *Makes approximately 8 cups*

Hollandaise Sauce III

NATHANIEL BURTON

5 egg yolks
3 ounces tarragon vinegar
3 ounces water

1 pound warm melted butter
Salt and cayenne pepper to
  taste

Combine egg yolks, vinegar, and water together in stainless-steel mixing bowl. Beat with wire whisk. Put in double boiler over simmering water until eggs have begun to thicken. Remove from fire. Gradually beat in warm butter, salt, and cayenne pepper. Blend and serve. *Makes 3 cups*

Louis Evans's Hollandaise Sauce
LOUIS EVANS

8 egg yolks
1 ounce water
1 ounce tarragon vinegar

1 pound butter
Dash of salt
Dash of Tabasco sauce

Place egg yolks, water, and vinegar in blender. Blend at a slow speed for 2 minutes. Turn off blender. Melt butter. Turn blender on and slowly pour butter over egg mixture. Add salt and Tabasco. *Makes 3 cups*

Oysters Rockefeller Sauce
HENRY CARR

½ bunch green onions, minced
2 ribs celery, minced
1 bunch parsley, minced
1 pound butter
½ cup breadcrumbs

1 ounce absinthe or Pernod
6 drops Tabasco sauce
¼ ounce Worcestershire sauce
Salt and pepper to taste

Combine green onions, celery, and parsley. Sauté mixture in butter. Add breadcrumbs, absinthe or Pernod, Tabasco, Worcestershire sauce, and salt and pepper. *Makes 2 cups—enough for 3 servings of 4 oysters each*

Bienville Sauce
AUSTIN LESLIE

¼ pound margarine
1 fish fillet (3-4 ounces, trout preferred), skin removed
¼ pound fresh shrimp (peeled and deveined)

¼ pound fresh lump crabmeat
6 egg whites, unbeaten
¼ cup white wine
1 teaspoon yellow food coloring
Salt and pepper to taste

Heat margarine in a large pot. Add fish, shrimp, and crabmeat. Sauté for 20 minutes. Add egg whites and stir. Add wine, continue stirring, and let simmer for 10 minutes. Add food coloring, salt, and pepper and stir for another 10 minutes. (Remember to stay with pot, don't leave!) Let cool and serve over Oysters Bienville (p. 109). *Serves 6*

The Original Rémoulade Sauce
SHERMAN CRAYTON

3 cups cooking oil
2 cups hot creole mustard
  (see Glossary, p. 316)
3 cups red vinegar
½ cup paprika

2 cups celery, chopped fine
1 cup parsley, chopped fine
2 cups green onions, chopped
  fine
Salt and pepper to taste

Mix oil, mustard, and vinegar and blend by hand for 15 to 20 minutes. Add paprika and stir. Mix in chopped ingredients, add salt and pepper to taste, and serve at room temperature or refrigerate for several hours. Serve over boiled shrimp, fish, or beef. (If sauce separates after refrigeration, shake to reblend ingredients.) *Makes 3 to 4 pints*

Rémoulade Sauce
CHARLES KIRKLAND

2 cups Mayonnaise (p. 244, or
  use ready-made)
¼ cup hot prepared mustard
¼ cup horseradish
1 teaspoon Tabasco sauce

2 stalks green onions,
  chopped finely
2 tablespoons Worcestershire
  sauce

Mix all ingredients. Stir well. *Makes 2½ cups*

Shrimp Sauce Rémoulade
LOUIS EVANS

French Dressing II (p. 245)

1 tablespoon prepared hot
   mustard

1 teaspoon prepared hot
   horseradish

6 shallots, chopped, or chives
   with tops

¼ teaspoon garlic salt

¼ teaspoon paprika

1½ pounds cooked shrimp,
   peeled

Make French Dressing. Add remaining ingredients, except shrimp, stirring each one in separately. Pour mixture over shrimp; mix thoroughly. Chill in refrigerator 30 minutes to 2 hours before using, so that the shrimp flavor permeates the sauce. *Makes 2 cups*

Rémoulade Sauce Creole
NATHANIEL BURTON

1 tablespoon dry mustard

3 tablespoons paprika

2 tablespoons salt

1 tablespoon sugar

1½ cups ketchup

4 cups vegetable oil

½ cup wine vinegar

½ cup horseradish

3 tablespoons chopped
   parsley

1½ bunch green onions, finely
   chopped

3 celery ribs, finely chopped

Put mustard, paprika, salt, and sugar in mixing bowl. Blend and add ketchup. Using wire whisk, blend in oil, vinegar, and horseradish and mix thoroughly. Add parsley, green onions, and celery. Mix well. Let stand at least 1 hour before using. *Makes 8 cups*

Rémoulade Sauce French
NATHANIEL BURTON

4 cups Mayonnaise (p. 244, or use ready-made)
1 bunch (½ cup) green onions, finely chopped
3 tablespoons chopped parsley
2 tablespoons dry mustard
2 tablespoons horseradish
4 tablespoons hot mustard
Chives

Put all ingredients in mixing bowl and blend thoroughly with whisk. Let chill in refrigerator at least an hour before using. Garnish with a pinch of fresh chives before serving. *Makes 4 cups*

Cocktail Sauce I
NATHANIEL BURTON

1 cup chili sauce (see Glossary, p. 315)
1 cup ketchup
¼ cup horseradish
Juice of 2 lemons

Put all ingredients in mixing bowl, mix thoroughly, and chill in refrigerator at least one hour before serving. *Makes 2 cups*

Cocktail Sauce II
CHARLES KIRKLAND

2 cups ketchup
¼ cup horseradish
¼ cup Worcestershire sauce
¼ cup vinegar
1 tablespoon Tabasco sauce

Mix all ingredients and stir well. *Makes about 2¾ cups*

Thousand Island Dressing I
HENRY CARR

4 cups Mayonnaise (p. 244, or ready-made)

1 cup chili sauce (see Glossary, p. 315)

2 teaspoons Worcestershire sauce

1 cup chopped pimento

4 hard-boiled eggs, chopped

Combine all ingredients in blender set at medium speed for 20 seconds. *Makes about 7 cups*

Thousand Island Dressing II
CHARLES KIRKLAND

½ cup chili sauce (see Glossary, p. 315)

1 hard-boiled egg, finely chopped

½ green bell pepper, finely chopped

2 stems green onions, finely chopped

2 cups Mayonnaise (p. 244, or use ready-made)

3 ounces (¼ cup) pimento, finely chopped

Mix all ingredients and stir well. *Makes about 3½ cups*

Mayonnaise
HENRY CARR

4 whole eggs

1 tablespoon dry mustard

Salt

1 ounce wine vinegar

6 cups peanut oil

Place eggs, mustard, salt, and vinegar into blender. Cover and blend at low speed for approximately five seconds. Turn speed control dial to #2 or medium speed. Remove cover and pour in the oil slowly, in a steady stream. When the mayonnaise has reached a smooth consistency, gradually increase speed until all of the oil has been added. Season to taste. If mayonnaise has to be stored, add 1 tablespoon of cold water and mix well. *Makes 7 cups*

French Dressing I
CHARLES KIRKLAND

2 cups vegetable oil (soybean preferably)
¼ cup white Bermuda onions, chopped

2 eggs
¼ cup vinegar
2 tablespoons salt

Stir and mix all ingredients. *Makes about 3 cups*

French Dressing II
LOUIS EVANS

1 tablespoon tarragon or basil vinegar
1 teaspoon salt
¼ teaspoon finely ground pepper

3 tablespoons olive oil
1 teaspoon prepared Creole mustard (see Glossary, p. 316)

Mix vinegar, salt, and pepper, beating thoroughly with fork. Blend oil with mustard, adding oil first drop by drop, then in small quantities, beating constantly. Add the vinegar, salt, and pepper solution, a few drops at a time, as the dressing appears to be curdling. (When the last of the oil and the last of the vinegar mixture have been whipped in, the dressing is ready to use as a base for the Shrimp Sauce Rémoulade [p. 242].) *Makes about ¼ cup*

Anchovy Dressing
NATHANIEL BURTON

2 tablespoons anchovy paste
1 cup French Dressing I (p. 245)
1 tablespoon chopped chives

Blend all ingredients thoroughly. *Makes about 1¼ cups dressing*

Tartar Sauce
NATHANIEL BURTON

1 cup Mayonnaise (p. 244, or
  ready-made)
¼ cup dill relish (pressed dry)
2 tablespoons capers, finely
  chopped

2 tablespoons parsley, finely
  chopped
2 tablespoons grated onion
1 tablespoon horseradish
1 teaspoon dry mustard

Put all ingredients in mixing bowl and blend thoroughly. Let sit
at least 30 minutes before using. *Makes 2 cups dressing*

Lummie Dressing
CHARLES BAILEY

1 egg
1 cup olive oil
3 ounces paprika
2 ounces dry mustard

Salt and pepper to taste
½ cup red vinegar
2 ounces blue cheese
1 tablespoon cornstarch

Blend ingredients at low speed in blender until smooth (25 to 30
minutes). The longer you whip it, the better it is. *Makes 1½ cups*

Vinaigrette Dressing
CHARLES KIRKLAND

2 cups vegetable oil
½ bunch green onions, finely
  chopped
¼ cup pickle relish

1 teaspoon paprika
¼ cup pimento, finely
  chopped
½ cup tarragon vinegar

Mix all ingredients and stir well. *Makes about 3 cups*

Fines Herbes Sauce
NATHANIEL BURTON

4 ounces butter
1 bunch green onions, finely
  chopped
12 fresh mushrooms,
  chopped
1 tablespoon fresh parsley,
  chopped

1 teaspoon fresh thyme, finely
  chopped
1 teaspoon oregano
4 cloves garlic, minced
4 cups Brown Sauce II (p. 233)
1 cup red wine
Juice of ½ lemon

Melt butter in a sauté pan or shallow skillet. Add onions, mushrooms, and parsley and sauté until dry. Add thyme, oregano, garlic, and brown sauce. Stir. Add the wine and cook about 30 minutes. Add lemon juice and serve with beef, veal, or poultry. *Makes about 4 cups*

Meunière Sauce I
LARRY WILLIAMSON

2 pounds butter
Juice of 3 fresh lemons and ½ teaspoon lemon concentrate
¼ cup wine vinegar

Brown butter lightly in 12-inch pot. Add lemon juice, then the vinegar. Stir over low flame for 10 minutes. *Makes 4 cups*

Meunière Sauce II
NATHANIEL BURTON

4 ounces butter
2 tablespoons fresh parsley, finely chopped
Juice of 2 lemons
1 tablespoon Worcestershire sauce

This sauce should never be prepared in advance. Brown butter in a skillet. Add the parsley, lemon juice, and Worcestershire sauce. Sauté for 30 seconds and serve at once, over sautéed fish. *Makes ½ cup*

Madeira Wine Sauce
NATHANIEL BURTON

2 ounces butter
6 fresh mushrooms, sliced
2 cups Brown Sauce I (p. 233)

½ cup Madeira
¼ cup Beef Stock (p. 213)

Melt butter in a skillet. Add mushrooms and brown them quickly on high heat for about 6 minutes. Add brown sauce, wine, and beef stock. Cook at least 10 minutes. Serve with beef, veal, or chicken. *Serves 6*

Fish Velouté Sauce
NATHANIEL BURTON

4 ounces butter
3 stalks green onions, finely
  chopped
6 fresh mushrooms, sliced

2 tablespoons flour
4 cups Fish Stock (p. 214)
¼ cup sherry

Melt butter in a saucepan. Add onions and mushrooms. Sauté until dry, approximately 6 to 7 minutes. Add flour and blend into a smooth roux, approximately 3 to 4 minutes. Cook over low heat. Do not brown. Add fish stock and sherry. Stir until smooth and let simmer for about 10 minutes. Serve with any poached fish. *Serves* 8

Mint Sauce
NATHANIEL BURTON

2 cups Brown Gravy I (p. 233)
6 fresh mint sprigs, finely chopped
6 tablespoons mint jelly

Put all ingredients in saucepan. Blend and let boil about 5 minutes. Serve with lamb chops. *Serves* 4

White Wine Sauce
NATHANIEL BURTON

4 tablespoons butter
6 fresh mushrooms, sliced
2 green onions, finely chopped
½ cup Fish Stock (p. 214)

½ cup white wine
2 cups Cream Sauce I (p. 234)
1 cup Hollandaise Sauce III
   (p. 239)

Put butter, mushrooms, and onions in saucepan and sauté until all moisture has evaporated. Add fish stock and white wine. Cook over high heat until liquid has reduced by half (approximately 10 minutes). Blend in cream sauce and hollandaise. Serve with seafood. *Serves* 8

Chasseur Sauce
NATHANIEL BURTON

4 ounces butter
4 green onions, finely chopped
1 cup mushrooms, sliced
4 slices bacon, cooked and diced
¾ cup sherry

1 cup tomatoes, crushed
1 tablespoon parsley, finely
   chopped
4 cups Brown Gravy I (p. 233)
6 tablespoons brandy

Melt butter in skillet. Add onions and mushrooms. Sauté until all moisture has evaporated. Add bacon, wine, tomatoes, parsley, and brown gravy and let cook at least 15 minutes. Add brandy immediately before serving. Serve with beef, chicken, or veal. *Serves* 8

Jardinière Sauce
NATHANIEL BURTON

4 tablespoons butter
5 fresh carrots, diced
½ cup green beans

½ cup green peas
½ cup small pearl onions
4 cups Brown Gravy I (p. 233)

Melt butter in saucepan. Add carrots and sauté slowly for 15 minutes. Add beans, peas, onions, and brown gravy. Let cook at least 20 minutes. Serve with beef, chicken, lamb, or veal. *Serves* 8

Marchand de Vin Sauce
NATHANIEL BURTON

4 ounces butter
4 green onions, finely chopped
1 dozen fresh mushrooms, sliced

4 cups Brown Gravy I (p. 233)
2 tablespoons parsley, chopped
1 cup red wine

Melt butter in saucepan. Add onions and mushrooms. Sauté until liquid evaporates (approximately 6 to 7 minutes). Add gravy, parsley, and red wine. Cook at least 20 minutes. Serve with beef, veal, or chicken. *Serves* 8

EGG DISHES

Ham and Eggs, Country Style
NATHANIEL BURTON

½ pound (2 sticks) butter
3 ham steaks, 1-inch thick, cut in half
1 dozen eggs

Melt butter in skillet. Fry ham steaks until browned. Crack 2 eggs on top of each ham steak; continue to cook until eggs are done, and serve. *Serves* 6

Egg and Veal Ricotta
NATHANIEL BURTON

4 ounces (1 stick) butter
Breadcrumbs
1 veal cutlet (about ¼ ounce)
6 tablespoons ricotta cheese
¼ cup tomato sauce

1 egg
¼ cup Mornay Sauce (p. 236)
2 tablespoons parmesan
   cheese, grated

Preheat broiler. Melt butter in skillet. Bread and sauté the veal cutlet. Combine ricotta and tomato sauce and put on plate next to cutlet. Poach one egg and place on top. Cover with Mornay sauce, sprinkle with parmesan, and glaze under the broiler. *Serves* 1

Creamed Turkey with Poached Eggs
NATHANIEL BURTON

2 cups cooked diced turkey
   breast
2 cups Cream Sauce I (p. 234)

8 fresh mushrooms, sliced
Salt and pepper
6 eggs

In saucepan, put turkey, cream sauce, mushrooms, and salt and pepper. Simmer on stove at least 10 minutes. Divide equally into 6 casseroles. Poach the eggs. Top each casserole with an egg and serve. *Serves* 6

Eggs and Luncheon Meat Special
NATHANIEL BURTON

6 hard-boiled eggs, coarsely
  chopped
¼ pound luncheon meat,
  finely chopped
2 tablespoons grated onion
1 teaspoon white pepper
½ cup Mayonnaise (p. 244, or
  ready-made)

1 cup cooked rice
1 cup Italian Breadcrumbs
  (p. 267)
1 cup tomato sauce
½ cup ricotta cheese

Preheat oven to 400°. In a mixing bowl, combine eggs, luncheon meat, onion, white pepper, mayonnaise, and rice. Mix thoroughly. Mold into 6 patties, roll in breadcrumbs, and place on a baking sheet. Bake for about 15 minutes. Meanwhile over low heat, combine tomato sauce and cheese. To serve, put one patty on each plate and cover with sauce. *Serves* 6

Eggs St. Denis
NATHANIEL BURTON

6 English muffins
1 dozen slices Canadian bacon
1 dozen eggs
3 cups Marchand de Vin Sauce (p. 251)

Split and toast English muffins and place on 6 plates. Grill bacon and put on muffins. Fry the eggs in hot bacon fat and place one egg on each muffin. Cover with Marchand de Vin sauce and serve. *Serves* 6

Eggs Benedict I

NATHANIEL BURTON

1 English muffin
2 slices Canadian bacon
2 eggs

¼ cup Hollandaise Sauce III
  (p. 239)
1 ripe black olive

Split muffin and toast. Put on plate. Grill bacon and place on muffin. Poach 2 eggs medium well and put on top of bacon. Cover with hollandaise sauce. Garnish with one half olive on each egg. *Serves* 1

Eggs Benedict II

MALCOM ROSS

Water for poaching
2 tablespoons vinegar
1 dozen eggs
2 pounds ham, cut into 6 slices

6 slices toasted bread
4 cups Hollandaise Sauce II
  (p. 239)

Heat water and vinegar in pan. When water is hot, break eggs about four or five at a time into the pan of water. Fry ham slices in separate pan. Put toast on plate when ready to serve. Put ham on top of toast, eggs on top of ham, and hollandaise sauce on eggs when ready to serve. *Serves* 6

Eggs Florentine
MALCOM ROSS

2 tablespoons vinegar
Enough water to poach eggs
8 eggs
1 pound frozen spinach or 2
cups finely chopped fresh
spinach

2 cups Cream Sauce II (p. 235)
½ cup breadcrumbs
4 tablespoons butter, melted

Preheat oven to 350°. Combine vinegar and water and heat. Break the eggs into the hot water (try not to break the yolks) and let cook 3 minutes. Remove from heat. In separate pot, cook spinach in boiling water for 6 minutes. Drain and add 6 tablespoons of the cream sauce. Divide the eggs and spinach between 4 ramekins or small individual casseroles, placing the spinach on the bottom followed by the eggs, 2 to each casserole. Top each with rest of cream sauce, breadcrumbs, and melted butter. Heat under broiler or in oven for 3 minutes. *Serves* 4

Fresh Tomatoes and Eggs
NATHANIEL BURTON

4 tablespoons butter
2 fresh ripe tomatoes
2 shallots, chopped
4 tablespoons Cheddar cheese

1 English muffin, split
2 slices Canadian bacon
2 eggs

Melt butter in skillet, add tomatoes and shallots. Cook about 10 minutes and add Cheddar cheese. Toast English muffin. Grill the bacon slices and place on the muffin. Poach two eggs lightly, put on top of the bacon. Cover with cheese-tomato mixture and serve. *Serves* 1

Fines Herbes Omelet
NATHANIEL BURTON

2 green onions, finely chopped
8 fresh mushrooms, finely
  chopped
1 tablespoon chopped parsley

6 ounces butter
1 dozen eggs
½ teaspoon oregano
½ teaspoon marjoram

Sauté onions, mushrooms, and chopped parsley in 2 ounces of the butter until tender. Break eggs in a bowl and add oregano and marjoram. Beat well. Melt remaining butter in another large pan. Add eggs and the onion mixture. Cook omelet until soft. Roll and serve. *Serves 6*

Chicken Liver Omelet
NATHANIEL BURTON

8 spring chicken livers
4 ounces (1 stick) butter
1 shallot, cut finely chopped

½ cup Brown Sauce I (p. 233)
3 eggs
Salt and pepper

Cut livers in half and sauté in pan with 2 ounces of the butter. When livers are browned, add shallot and brown sauce. Crack eggs in bowl and beat well. Add salt and pepper. Melt remaining butter in another pan. Add eggs and let set. Fold in half of the livers. Serve omelet on plate and garnish with remaining chicken livers. *Serves 2*

Crabmeat Omelet I
BON TON

1 bunch green onions, finely
  chopped
½ stick butter
½ teaspoon salt

½ teaspoon black pepper
5 tablespoons crabmeat
4 eggs

Sauté green onions in ¼ stick of the butter. Add salt and pepper. Fold in crabmeat. Cook 5 minutes. Melt remaining butter in a heavy skillet and use 2 eggs for each omelet. Fold in 2½ tablespoons crabmeat mixture for each omelet. *Serves* 2

Crabmeat Omelet II
NATHANIEL BURTON

1 stick butter   ¼ cup Cream Sauce I (p. 234)
1 green onion, finely chopped   3 eggs
4 tablespoons fresh crabmeat   Salt and pepper

Melt half the butter in skillet and add green onion. Cook for 2 minutes. Add crabmeat and cream sauce and cook for 5 minutes. Crack eggs in bowl and beat well. Melt remaining butter and when warm, add eggs, salt, and pepper and fold in half of the crabmeat. Put omelet on plate and garnish with remaining crabmeat. *Serves* 1

Egg and Cheese Casserole
NATHANIEL BURTON

¼ cup Mayonnaise (p. 244, or   1 teaspoon Worcestershire
   use ready-made)   sauce
1 cup grated Cheddar cheese   6 eggs
¼ teaspoon salt   4 tablespoons grated parme-
½ teaspoon white pepper   san cheese
¼ cup half-and-half or light
   cream

Preheat oven to 350°. Combine mayonnaise, Cheddar cheese, salt, pepper, half-and-half, and Worcestershire sauce in a saucepan. Stir and heat slowly until cheese melts. Cover the bottoms of 6 casseroles with cheese sauce. Crack one egg into each casserole. Pour more sauce over egg. Sprinkle with parmesan cheese and bake 15 to 20 minutes. *Serves 6*

Eggs and Lobster
NATHANIEL BURTON

4 tablespoons (½ stick) butter
4 shallots, finely chopped
6 ripe tomatoes, finely
    chopped
½ cup Cheddar cheese
Salt
White pepper
3 14-ounce lobster tails,
    boiled and diced
4 tablespoons sherry
1 dozen eggs

Melt butter in skillet and add shallots and cook until tender. Add tomatoes and cook slowly until done. Stir in cheese and when melted, add salt, pepper, lobster meat, and sherry. Simmer over low heat about 10 minutes. Poach eggs lightly and place 2 eggs in each of 6 casserole dishes or ramekins. Cover with the lobster sauce and serve. *Serves 6*

Eggs and Oysters in Patty Shells
NATHANIEL BURTON

2 tablespoons butter
1 bunch green onions, finely
    chopped (about ¾ cup)
1 quart oysters, drained
2 cups Cream Sauce I (p. 234)
Salt and white pepper to taste
6 eggs, poached
6 large patty shells
2 tablespoons chopped parsley

Put butter and onions in skillet and cook until tender. Add drained oysters. Cook until oysters curl at edges. Add cream sauce, salt, and pepper. Simmer at least 10 minutes. Poach the eggs (medium). Pour a spoonful of oyster mixture into each patty shell. Then add a poached egg and top with another spoon of oysters. Sprinkle each shell with parsley and serve. *Serves* 6

Eggs and Shrimp Newburg
NATHANIEL BURTON

2 pounds fresh shrimp, peeled and deveined	3 egg yolks
	Salt and pepper
6 tablespoons sherry	¼ cup brandy
2 cups Cream Sauce I (p. 234)	1 dozen whole eggs

Preheat oven to 350°. Boil shrimp and drain. Heat gently with sherry and cream sauce for 5 minutes. Beat 3 egg yolks with salt and pepper. Mix in the brandy and add the egg mixture to the shrimp and cream sauce. Blend thoroughly and keep it warm. Do not let it boil. Place eggs in 6 casseroles, two eggs in each, and bake in a 350° oven until eggs are set. Remove eggs from oven and top with shrimp mixture. *Serves* 6

BREAD, CRÊPES, AND NEW ORLEANS SPECIALTIES

French Bread

NATHANIEL BURTON

½ cup milk
1 cake yeast
5 cups sifted flour
1½ cups water

1 tablespoon sugar
1 teaspoon salt
1 tablespoon butter

Preheat oven to 375°. Scald milk and let stand until it gets luke-warm. Add yeast to milk. Mix flour, water, sugar, salt, and butter together in large bowl. Add yeast and milk mixture to flour mixture. Cover dough with a cloth and let it rise in a warm place for 2 hours. Dough will double in size. Remove dough to table and knead for 5 minutes. Grease a baking sheet. Divide dough and shape into three loaves. Place on sheet pan and let it double in size a second time. Bake at least 25 minutes. *Makes 3 loaves*

Lost Bread, or Pain Perdu

NATHANIEL BURTON

2 eggs
¼ cup sugar
1 cup milk
1 tablespoon vanilla extract

1 teaspoon cinnamon
4 ounces (1 stick) butter
4 slices stale bread

Beat together eggs and sugar. Add milk, vanilla, and cinnamon and blend thoroughly. Melt butter in skillet. Trim edges from bread and cut into triangles. Soak each piece in the egg mixture and sauté until golden brown. Serve with jelly or top with confectioners' sugar. *Serves 2*

Dinner Rolls I
ANNIE LAURA SQUALLS

1½ teaspoons salt

2½ cups sifted flour

3 tablespoons sugar

4 tablespoons granulated yeast

¼ cup warm water

2 tablespoons butter

3 tablespoons vegetable
   shortening

2 eggs

1 cup milk

Preheat oven to 450°. Sift dry ingredients. Dissolve yeast in water. In a large bowl, cream butter, shortening, and eggs together. Stir in yeast mixture. Gradually add milk, alternating with flour mixture. Mix well. Cover dough and let rise in warm place for half an hour. Punch down dough to release air and let it rise again. Roll out dough and shape into rolls. Bake in oven for 10 to 15 minutes. *Makes 1 dozen rolls*

Dinner Rolls II
NATHANIEL BURTON

½ cup milk

2 cakes yeast

5 cups flour

1½ tablespoons salt

¼ cup sugar

2 ounces butter

2 cups water

Preheat oven to 375°. Scald milk and let stand until lukewarm. Add yeast to milk. Mix flour, salt, sugar, butter, and water together in large bowl. Add yeast to flour mixture. Cover with a cloth and let rise in a warm place. Dough will double in size in approximately 40 minutes. Punch down dough. Divide into 24 pieces. Place each piece of dough in well of a lightly greased muffin pan. Let rise again. Bake for 15 minutes. *Makes 2 dozen rolls*

Biscuits
CORINNE DUNBAR'S

2 cups flour
1 tablespoon baking powder
3 tablespoons sugar
2 teaspoons salt

¾ cup milk
5 tablespoons shortening
Melted butter

Preheat oven to 450°. Mix all dry ingredients together in a large bowl. Stir in milk and shortening. Sprinkle additional flour on board. Roll out dough to ¼-inch thickness. Cut into 25 2½-inch circles and lay on greased cookie sheet. Brush tops with melted butter. Bake for 10 minutes. *Makes 25 large biscuits*

Breadcrumbs
NATHANIEL BURTON

Grate 4 slices of hard stale bread. If stale bread is not available, use fresh bread dried out in a 350° oven. Turn bread frequently while in oven; do not let it brown. Breadcrumbs can also be made in a mixer. *Makes 1 cup*

Italian Breadcrumbs
NATHANIEL BURTON

2 cups fine breadcrumbs
2 ounces grated parmesan
    cheese
1 tablespoon oregano
1 tablespoon marjoram

1 tablespoon sweet basil
2 tablespoons chives, finely
    chopped
2 tablespoons parsley, chopped

Mix all ingredients. Use for frying fish, veal, or chicken. *Makes about 2 cups crumbs*

Beignets (French Doughnuts)
NATHANIEL BURTON

1 cup half-and-half	5 cups flour
1 cup sugar	1 teaspoon mace
1 cake yeast	Oil for deep-frying
2 eggs, beaten	Confectioners' sugar
½ pound (2 sticks) butter, melted	

Combine half-and-half and sugar in a saucepan. Place over a medium flame until barely heated through. Do not bring to a boil. Remove from stove. Crumble cake yeast into beaten eggs and fold into milk and sugar mixture. Slowly pour in the melted butter. Stir. Add flour and mace all at once and mix well. Let stand in a warm place at least 2 hours, until risen. Roll dough out to 1-inch thickness on floured board and cut into squares. Let stand until dough rises again to double in bulk. Deep-fry at 300° for about 6 minutes. Drain and sprinkle with confectioners' sugar. *Makes 2 dozen*

French Pancakes Cordon Bleu
HENRY CARR

1 cup half-and-half	5 cups flour
1 cup sugar	1 teaspoon mace
1 cake yeast	Oil for deep-frying
2 eggs, beaten	Confectioners' sugar
½ pound (2 sticks) butter, melted	

Preheat oven to 350°. Make crêpes and set aside. Cook spinach in a small amount of water until tender. Drain and chop coarsely. Mix with butter and seasonings. Arrange the crêpes on a table, light side up. Place 1 slice of cheese on each crêpe and cover with 1 slice of ham. Mound a small amount of spinach in the center and cover with another slice of ham. Fold crêpes over and arrange them side by side in a shallow ovenproof dish. Put the dish in a 350° oven for a few minutes. Before serving, coat each crêpe with the Mornay sauce and glaze under the broiler. *Serves 6*

Crêpes I
LOUIS EVANS

1 cup flour
1 ounce liquid shortening
2 whole eggs

1 ounce vanilla extract
1 cup half-and-half
2 cups homogenized milk

Mix flour, shortening, eggs, vanilla, half-and-half and milk into a smooth batter. Pour about ¼ cup of batter onto a hot, well-oiled crepe pan or small frying pan. Turn pan so batter will spread out. Brown on one side. *Makes 8 crêpes*

Crêpes II
NATHANIEL BURTON

2 whole eggs
¼ cup flour
1 teaspoon salt
1 ounce cooking oil (plus oil
　for frying)

1 tablespoon vanilla extract
1 cup milk

Mix eggs into the flour. Add salt, oil, and vanilla. Mix well. Add milk and beat until smooth. Pour small amount of batter onto a hot, oiled, 8-inch frying pan or crepe pan. Brown on both sides over high flame. Remove from pan, cover with towel, and set aside. *Makes 8 crêpes*

Crêpes Maritimes
SHERMAN CRAYTON

1 cup green onions, finely
   chopped
1 cup celery, chopped
2 ounces butter
¼ pound crabmeat, drained
¼ pound cooked shrimp,
   chopped

6 Crêpes I (p. 269)
½ cup Cream Sauce I (p. 234)
4 ounces grated parmesan
   cheese

Preheat oven to 350°. Sauté green onions and celery in butter for
10 minutes. Add crabmeat and shrimp to onion-celery mixture
and sauté for another 5 minutes. Place mixture on crêpes, fold
over and top with cream sauce and cheese. Bake until brown
(approximately 15 minutes). *Serves* 6

French Pancakes Bonne Femme
HENRY CARR

1 dozen Crêpes I (p. 269)
2 ounces unsalted butter
1 small onion, finely chopped
6 good-sized fresh mush-
   rooms, sliced
1 teaspoon salt
Freshly ground pepper

2 cups dry white wine
2 cups Fish Stock (p. 214)
1 teaspoon fresh parsley,
   chopped
6 8-ounce fillets of flounder
½ cup Béchamel Sauce (p. 236)

Preheat oven to 350°. Prepare crêpes and set aside. Melt the
butter in a large saucepan. Add the onion, mushrooms, salt and
pepper, wine, fish stock, and parsley. Add the fish fillets and let
cook, covered, for 6 to 8 minutes. Remove the fish fillets from
the cooking broth, drain well, divide, and place in the center
of the crêpes. Reduce the cooking liquid by ⅓ of its original

quantity. Add the béchamel sauce to the reduced cooking liquid and correct the seasoning. Pour an equal amount of sauce on each crêpe. Fold the crêpes and place, seam side down, in an ovenproof dish. Heat in a 350° oven for 8 minutes before serving. *Makes 6 2-crêpe servings*

Crab Crêpes Bengal
ROCHESTER ANDERSON

6 thin Crêpes I, browned on 1 side only (p. 269)

Whipped-Cream Sauce
1 egg yolk
⅛ teaspoon salt

4 tablespoons butter, melted
2 teaspoons lemon juice
½ cup Cream Sauce I (p. 234)
¼ cup heavy cream, whipped

Beat egg yolk with salt and add to it 2 tablespoons of the warm melted butter, bit by bit. Mix the remaining melted butter with the lemon juice and add it to the egg mixture, beating constantly. Stir in the cream sauce and fold in the whipped cream.

Crêpe Filling
1 tablespoon butter
3 teaspoons chopped shallots
3 cups lump crabmeat
1 teaspoon curry powder
Salt to taste
⅛ teaspoon pepper

Dash cayenne
¼ teaspoon Worcestershire sauce
½ cup white wine
1 cup Cream Sauce I (p. 234)

Preheat oven to 350°. Melt butter in a skillet. Lightly sauté the chopped shallots. Add the crabmeat. Season this mixture with curry powder, salt, pepper, cayenne, and Worcestershire. Add the wine and simmer and stir for 3 minutes. Add the cream sauce and blend well. Put 3 tablespoons of the crab mixture on the browned side of each crêpe. Roll the crêpes and arrange them in a baking dish, topped with the whipped-cream sauce. Put the dish under the broiler, set at 350°, until crêpes are golden brown. Serve at once. *Serves* 6

Crêpes au Curry

LOUIS EVANS

3 chicken breasts, skinned
   and boned
4 cups Chicken Stock (p. 213)
¼ teaspoon chicken base or 1
   bouillon cube
3 pineapple slices
2 bananas cut into ¾-inch
   pieces

3 tablespoons butter
1 cup flour
½ tablespoon curry powder
Salt
White pepper
6 Crêpes I (p. 269)

Preheat oven to 450°. Boil chicken breasts in chicken stock combined with the chicken base or bouillon cube until tender. Remove chicken from pot and cut into small pieces. Combine pineapple and bananas and return to stock. Let stand for 5 minutes until bananas have softened. Remove and set aside with chicken pieces while making sauce:

In another pan cook butter and flour for 3 minutes; add chicken stock, curry powder, salt, and pepper and cook for 10 more minutes. Prepare crêpes according to directions. Stuff each crêpe with the chicken and banana-pineapple mixture. Cover crêpes with curry sauce and heat in oven for 3 to 5 minutes before serving. *Serves* 6

Crêpe Soufflé I

NATHANIEL BURTON

2 whole eggs
¼ cup flour
1 teaspoon salt
1 ounce cooking oil (plus oil for flying)
1 tablespoon vanilla
1 cup milk
8 egg whites
1 pound confectioners' sugar
1 teaspoon pistachio flavoring
1 teaspoon yellow food coloring

Rind of 1 orange, grated
1 cup granulated sugar plus 2 tablespoons
6 egg yolks
1½ cups half-and-half or light cream
1 teaspoon mace
3 ounces Myers rum (or any Jamaican rum)

Preheat oven to 500°. Mix 2 whole eggs with flour. Add salt, oil, and vanilla. Mix and add cup of milk. Cook crêpe batter in oiled 8-inch frying pan or crêpe pan over high flame. Makes 8 crêpes. Cover with towel and set aside. Beat egg whites until stiff. Add confectioners' sugar, pistachio flavoring, and food coloring and beat with wire whip. Add grated orange rind and mix in. Lay crêpes flat and spoon filling on each. Fold and place on baking sheet. Sprinkle with 2 tablespoons of sugar and bake 6 minutes.

Cream egg yolks and rest of granulated sugar. Add half-and-half or light cream. Cook in double boiler until thick. Remove from stove and add mace and rum. Serve over crêpes. *Serves* 8 (1 *crêpe per serving*)

Crêpe Soufflé II
LOUIS EVANS

1 cup flour
1 ounce liquid shortening
2 whole eggs
1 ounce vanilla extract
2 cups half-and-half
2 cups homogenized milk
6 egg whites

¾ pound confectioners' sugar
Rind of 1 orange, grated
5 egg yolks
½ cup granulated sugar
1 teaspoon mace
2 ounces dark Bacardi rum

Preheat oven to 400°. To make crêpes, mix flour, shortening, whole eggs, vanilla, 1 cup of the half-and-half, and the homogenized milk into a batter. Brown on a griddle, in crêpe pan, or small fry pan.

To make filling, mix egg whites with confectioners' sugar, using an eggbeater or wire whisk to beat to a meringue texture. Add orange rind and beat until the mixture expands. Beat for an additional 10 minutes until dry and stiff peaks form. Fold into crêpes and place in oven for 10 minutes. They will rise like a soufflé. To make the sauce, put egg yolks, granulated sugar, mace, and remainder of the half-and-half in a double boiler. Stir constantly for 10 to 15 minutes until sauce has thickened. Add rum. When crêpes have risen, remove from oven and arrange on serving plates. Cover with sauce and serve. *Makes* 8 *crêpes*

Crêpes Brulatour
NATHANIEL BURTON

12 Crêpes II (p. 269)
1 pound cream cheese (at room temperature)
1 cup sugar

½ cup pecans, chopped
1 ounce half-and-half (or light cream)
2 teaspoons vanilla

Filling
Put cream cheese, sugar, pecans, and half-and-half into a mixing bowl and blend well. Stir in vanilla. Chill for half an hour. Place a spoonful of the chilled cream cheese mixture on each crêpe and roll up.

Sauce

4 ounces (1 stick) butter
1 quart sliced strawberries
2 ounces cherry-flavored liqueur (optional)*

2 ounces strawberry liqueur
2 cups whipped cream
½ cup Melba sauce

Put butter in a chafing dish, add strawberries, and heat. Add crêpes, let simmer until hot, about 5 minutes. Combine cherry-flavored and strawberry liqueurs and flame. Serve on a warm plate. Top with strawberries, whipped cream, and Melba sauce. *Serves* 6

*If both liqueurs are used, limit each amount to 2 ounces, i.e., do not use more than 4 ounces of liqueur. If only one liqueur is used, measure 4 ounces.

Crêpes with Blueberry Sauce
HENRY CARR

8 Crêpes I (p. 269)
2 cups pastry cream (see below)

½ cup blueberry jelly
½ stick butter
1¾ cups Marsala

Preheat oven to 350°. Fill crêpes with pastry cream. Roll up and place on heatproof silver platter and heat in oven for 5 minutes. Combine jelly, butter, and wine and cook until thick. Pour sauce over warm crêpes. *Serves* 4

Pastry Cream

2 ounces (½ stick) butter,
   melted
¼ cup flour

2 cups half-and-half
½ cup sugar
2 tablespoons vanilla (pure)

Melt butter in saucepan. Blend with flour for 5 minutes. Scald half-and-half and add to roux. Stir until smooth. Add sugar and vanilla and let sit on top of warm stove for at least 5 minutes. Remove from heat and let cool. Then use for filling. *Makes 2¼ cups*

Apple-Stuffed Crêpes Normandy
HENRY CARR

2 pounds Yellow Delicious
   apples (2 cups when sliced)
1¼ cups sugar
¼ pound (1 stick) unsalted or
   sweet butter (cut in pieces)
1 ounce cognac or applejack

1 cup whipped cream
12 Crêpes I (p. 269)
2 cups vanilla ice cream,
   melted at room temperature
   (do not heat)

Preheat oven to 350°. Peel the apples, removing the cores. Cut each apple into 8 to 10 wedges. Place in blender for 10 seconds at medium speed. Put the sugar in a skillet and heat moderately, stirring with a wooden spatula until the sugar turns golden. Add the butter and cook until melted. Add apples, then the cognac or applejack. Cook slowly, stirring constantly, for 12 to 15 minutes or until the apples are soft but not mushy. Remove from stove and blend in the whipped cream. Arrange crêpes light side up. Place apple mixture in center of each, then roll up. Prior to serving, place the crêpes on a heatproof buttered serving dish. Bake for a few minutes at 350°. Spoon melted vanilla ice cream over each portion before serving. *Serves 6*

Cherry Heering Crêpes Jubilee
HENRY CARR

2 cans (approximately 1 pound each) pitted dark sweet cherries in heavy syrup
1 tablespoon cornstarch
½ cup water
2 ounces Cherry Heering liqueur
12 small scoops of vanilla or cherry burgundy ice cream
1 dozen Crêpes I (p. 269)

Strain the cherries, reserving juice. Pour juice into a skillet and bring to a boil. Dilute cornstarch in the water and add it to the boiling juice. Cook for 2 minutes, beating with a wire whisk. Remove from stove. Add liqueur and cherries and keep warm until ready to serve. Place 1 scoop of ice cream in center of each crêpe. Fold crêpes over the ice cream. Spoon the cherry mixture over each portion. *Serves 6 (2 crêpes per serving)*

Oyster Dressing
NATHANIEL BURTON

1 pound pork sausage meat, ground
1 medium onion, finely chopped
2 ribs celery, finely chopped
1 green bell pepper, finely chopped
1 quart oysters
1 loaf stale French bread
Salt and pepper to taste

Preheat oven to 400°. Cook pork sausage in skillet until brown and almost completely dry. Remove from pan and set aside. Add vegetables to sausage drippings and cook until tender. Mix together sausage and vegetables. Scald oysters and drain. Wet bread thoroughly, then squeeze out excess water. Tear damp bread into pieces. Add oysters and bread pieces to sausage and vegetable mixture. Mix together and season with salt and pepper. Bake in a 400° oven at least 20 minutes. *Makes 8 cups*

Hot Sausage Sandwich on French Bread
LEAH CHASE

Water
Creole hot sausage (see Glossary, p. 316)
Hot French bread

Barely cover bottom of skillet with water. Add sausage, cover and cook for 10 minutes. Remove cover and brown sausage on all sides. Serve on hot French bread, with lettuce, sliced tomatoes, and mayonnaise (optional).

Boiled Pickled Pork with Turnips and Greens
NATHANIEL BURTON

1 5-pound pickled pork butt (see Glossary, p. 317)
3 bunches of turnips with their greens
1 onion, finely chopped
4 ounces shortening

Put pork in pot and cover with cold water. Bring to a boil and simmer at least 3 hours. Drain off half the pork stock and set aside. Slice pork and return to remaining stock until ready to serve. Wash greens and peel turnips. Put together in a pot, cover with half water and half pork stock. Bring to a boil. Sauté onion in shortening until tender and add greens. Cook at least 2 hours. *Serves 6*

Red Beans
AUSTIN LESLIE

1 pound red beans
2 medium onions, diced
1 rib celery, diced
1 clove garlic, finely chopped
4 sprigs parsley, chopped

1 pound pickled pork rib tips
  (see Glossary, p. 317) or
  smoked shoulder of ham,
  cubed, or smoked ham hocks
Salt and pepper to taste
4 cups cooked rice

Pick over beans before cleaning and remove any bruised or spotted ones. Soak in water overnight in a covered pot. Add diced onions to beans while they are soaking. The following day, strain and pour off water. Return beans and onions to pot. Fill ¾ full of water. Add celery, garlic, parsley, and pickled meat. Cook over a medium flame. Season to taste. Reduce flame as necessary to simmer for 2½ to 3 hours. Serve over boiled rice. *Serves 6*

Red Beans and Rice
NATHANIEL BURTON

1 pound red beans
2 cloves garlic, finely chopped
6 cups cold water
2 bay leaves
4 tablespoons bacon drippings
Salt and pepper

1 large onion, finely
  chopped
½ pound pickled pork, diced
  (see Glossary, p. 317)
1 green bell pepper, finely
  chopped

Wash beans in cold water. Drain beans and put in covered pot with the cold water. Bring to a boil slowly. Put drippings in a skillet, add onion, green pepper, garlic, bay leaves, and salt and pepper. Cook until tender. Add vegetables to beans and cook at least 1 hour, then add pickled pork and cook for 1 more hour. Serve with rice. *Serves 6*

Red Kidney Beans with Pickled Pork
LEAH CHASE

1 pound red kidney beans
2 quarts water
2 medium onions, chopped
1 pound pickled pork, cut in
  cubes (see Glossary, p. 317)

½ cup cooking oil
1 bay leaf
2 cloves garlic, minced
2 sprigs parsley, chopped
Salt and pepper to taste

Wash and soak beans overnight. Drain. Cover beans with water and boil for 1 hour on slow flame. Add onions and pickled pork and cook until tender. Add oil, bay leaf, garlic, and parsley. Add salt and pepper to taste. Cook about half an hour. Serve over rice. In New Orleans, we serve this dish with hot sausage. *Serves 6*

Fried Grits
CORINNE DUNBAR'S

3 cups uncooked hominy grits
4 cups water
½ teaspoon salt
1 teaspoon baking powder
3 eggs, beaten
½ cup butter

Pinch of flour
½ teaspoon sugar
4 eggs
½ cup milk
Shortening

Cook grits in boiling water in saucepan for 15 minutes with salt and baking powder. Whip in beaten eggs. Stir in butter, flour, and sugar and cook for 15 minutes. Pour mixture in shallow pan to a depth of 1 inch and refrigerate overnight. Cut grits in 3-inch squares. Mix remaining eggs and milk together to make egg wash. Dip squares in egg wash and fry in shortening until golden brown. *Serves 6*

Spaghettini and Shallots

HENRY CARR

Water
Salt
1 pound spaghettini
¼ pound or 1 stick butter

1 cup chopped shallots
¼ cup chopped parsley
Salt and pepper to taste

Fill a 4-quart pot ¾ full of water. Add salt and bring to a boil. Drop spaghettini into rapidly boiling water and stir to keep from sticking together. Heat butter over low flame in saucepan with shallots and parsley. Do not cook shallots until limp, just heat through. Entire cooking time should not exceed 6 to 8 minutes. Drain spaghettini and place on 4 9"-plates. Cover with shallot sauce and add salt and pepper to taste. *Serves* 4

Oysters in Spaghetti

NATHANIEL BURTON

4 ounces butter
3 shallots, finely chopped
1 rib celery, finely chopped
Pepper to taste
2 dozen fresh oysters
4 cloves garlic, minced

2 tablespoons chopped
  parsley
1 cup Cream Sauce I (p. 234)
1 gallon water
1 pound #3 spaghetti

Melt butter in skillet. Add shallots, celery, and pepper and sauté until tender. Drain oysters. Reserve oyster water. Add garlic and oysters to pan. Cook for 5 or 6 minutes. Add 1 tablespoon of the parsley. Add oyster water and cream sauce. Cook 5 or 6 minutes and set aside. Bring 1 gallon water to boil. Add spaghetti and cook for 6 minutes, stirring to keep strands from sticking together. Drain and serve with sauce. Use remaining parsley to garnish. *Serves* 4

Chicken Livers with Spaghetti
NATHANIEL BURTON

2 ounces (½ a stick) butter
2 dozen spring chicken livers
Salt and pepper to taste
1 pint commercial marinara
    sauce or commercial
    tomato sauce

1 gallon water
1 pound #3 spaghetti

Melt butter in skillet. Add chicken livers and brown on both sides. Salt and pepper to taste. Add marinara sauce or tomato sauce and simmer at least 10 minutes. Bring 1 gallon salted water to boil in pot. Add spaghetti and stir to keep strands from sticking together. Cook 6 minutes and drain. Serve livers with spaghetti. *Serves* 4

Baked Lasagna
HENRY CARR

1 package # 13 large lasagna,
    cooked
2 green bell peppers, diced
2 large onions, diced
4 ribs celery, diced
4 cloves garlic, minced
1 tablespoon cooking oil
1 small can sliced mushrooms
2 sprigs parsley, chopped

Salt and pepper to taste
½ pound ground beef
1 quart tomato sauce
¼ pound ricotta cheese
1 egg
4 hard-boiled eggs, chopped
1 pound mozzarella cheese,
    sliced

Preheat oven to 350°. Cook and drain lasagna according to package directions. Sauté peppers, onions, celery, and garlic in cooking oil. Add mushrooms, parsley, and salt and pepper. Stir in ground beef and sauté for a half hour. Add one pint of the tomato sauce. Spread some additional tomato sauce on bottom of 8" x 12" baking pan. Put one layer of lasagna in pan, overlapping sides. Spread on a layer of meat sauce. Mix ricotta cheese and raw egg together. Spread on top of meat sauce. Add a layer of hard-boiled eggs and mozzarella cheese. Fold lasagna up over sides and lay the remaining pieces of lasagna across the top lengthwise. Spread on remaining tomato sauce and mozzarella cheese. Bake for 35 minutes. *Serves* 12

Bouillabaisse Marseillaise à la Creole
SHERMAN CRAYTON

2 bay leaves
3 green bell peppers, sliced
3 medium white onions, sliced
4 celery ribs, sliced
2 cloves garlic, chopped
1 bunch green onions, chopped
½ cup cooking oil
2 #2 cans tomatoes (crushed)
2 quarts water
1 lemon (cut in half)

½ pound redfish fillet, cut in bite-size pieces
½ pound fresh jumbo shrimp, peeled and deveined
1 dozen oysters
½ pound fresh lump crabmeat
Pinch of saffron
1 cup white wine
Salt
Pepper

Place bay leaves, peppers, onions, celery, garlic, and green onions in a 2-quart pot and sauté in cooking oil for 10 minutes. Add tomatoes, water, and lemon. Sauté redfish, shrimp, oysters, and crabmeat (or as many kinds of fish or seafood as desired). (Instead of sautéing, fish can be baked in oven for 10 minutes at 300°.) Place sautéed fish and shrimp in soup. Cook over low flame for 45 minutes, then add crabmeat and oysters. Cook a few minutes more. Add saffron, wine, and salt and pepper. Remove lemon before serving. *Serves* 6

Bouillabaisse à la Creole

RAYMOND THOMAS, SR.

2 quarts Fish Stock (p. 214)
1 pound redfish, cubed or in bite-size pieces
½ lobster tail (cubed)
1 pound shrimp, shelled and deveined
1 pint oysters
1 10-ounce can whole tomatoes, mashed
Pinch of saffron
Salt and pepper to taste

Bring all ingredients to a boil in a 1-gallon pot. Lower flame and simmer for a half hour and serve. *Serves 4 to 6*

Creole Jambalaya

LEAH CHASE

1 slice smoked ham, ½" thick, cubed
¼ pound smoked sausage, cut in ½" pieces
¼ pound hot link sausage, cut in ½" pieces
1 cup chopped white onion
1 green bell pepper, finely chopped
2 cups uncooked rice
½ teaspoon paprika
1 teaspoon salt
1 tablespoon fresh parsley, chopped
1 teaspoon ground thyme
2 cups boiling water

Put ham, sausages, onions, and green pepper in 3-quart saucepan. Cover and cook over medium heat until vegetables are soft. (Meat will provide enough fat for cooking.) Add rice, paprika, salt, parsley, and thyme. Stir and cook for 5 minutes. Add the boiling water. Increase flame. Bring to a boil and let boil 5 minutes. Stir, then cover tightly. Lower fire and cook until rice is tender, about 35 minutes. *Serves 6*

Shrimp Jambalaya
RAYMOND THOMAS, SR.

2 medium-size white onions, finely chopped
1 green bell pepper, finely chopped
1 bunch green onions, finely chopped
1 rib celery, finely chopped
1 clove garlic, minced
1 bay leaf
1 cup oil
1 10-ounce can whole tomatoes
1 10-ounce can tomato sauce
1½ pounds raw, medium shrimp (peeled and deveined)
1 pound rice

Preheat oven to 350°. Sauté chopped vegetables, garlic, and bay leaf in cooking oil for 5 minutes. Add tomatoes and tomato sauce and cook for 15 minutes. Add shrimp and cook for 10 minutes. Cook rice in a separate pot and add to shrimp and sauce. Put mixture in roasting pan or casserole and bake for 3 to 5 minutes at 350°. *Serves 4 to 6*

Gumbo z'Herbes*
CORINNE DUNBAR'S

1 bunch collard greens
1 bunch mustard greens
1 bunch turnip greens
1 bunch spinach
1 bunch watercress
1 bunch beet tops
1 bunch carrot tops
1 bunch parsley
1 bunch chicory
1 bunch radish tops
1 green cabbage
½ bunch green onions
1 gallon water, salted
1 pound boiled ham, diced
1 pound lean veal, diced
2 tablespoons shortening
1 large white onion, chopped
1 tablespoon parsley, chopped
2 bay leaves
4 sprigs thyme
2 whole cloves
2 whole allspice
Salt and pepper to taste
Cayenne to taste

Wash all greens thoroughly and remove all stems or hard centers. Boil them all together in the water for about 2 hours. Strain the greens and save the water. Chop the greens finely. Sauté ham and veal in shortening for about 10 minutes in a deep iron skillet. Add onion and chopped parsley and sauté until onion is brown. Add greens and simmer 15 minutes. Add contents of skillet to water from the greens. Add bay leaves, thyme, cloves, allspice, salt, pepper, and cayenne. Cook over a low flame for 1 hour. *Serves* 10 *to* 12

* Precision measuring is never done in this gumbo.

Salad Lummie
CHARLES BAILEY

Salt and pepper
24 fresh artichoke hearts, sliced, or 2 cans of artichoke hearts
Favorite salad dressing
1 head lettuce, chopped or shredded
1 pound cooked shrimp
2 fresh peeled grapefruits, sectioned or sliced
3 fresh peeled oranges, sectioned or sliced

Salt and pepper artichoke hearts to taste. Toss in salad dressing. Place artichoke hearts on bed of shredded lettuce. Place shrimp on top of artichoke hearts and arrange fruit around shrimp. *Serves* 8

Crabmeat Salad
CHARLES KIRKLAND

3 hard-boiled eggs, chopped
3 celery ribs, chopped
¼ cup Mayonnaise (p. 244, or ready-made)
Salt and pepper to taste
1 pound fresh lump crabmeat

Combine all ingredients except crabmeat in a bowl. Top with crabmeat and fold over, being careful not to break up crab. Be sure to go easy on the mayonnaise so the delicate flavor of the crabmeat will come through. *Serves 4*

Shrimp Salad

CHARLES KIRKLAND

1½ pounds shrimp (shells intact)	*For boiling shrimp*
3 ribs celery, finely chopped	½ lemon
3 green onions, finely chopped	2 green onions, chopped
3 hard-boiled eggs	1 rib celery, chopped
¾ cup Mayonnaise (p. 244, or ready-made)	1 tablespoon cayenne pepper
	Salt to taste
Salt and pepper to taste	Water

Boil shrimp for 5 minutes in pot with lemon, onions, celery, cayenne, salt, and water. Drain shrimp and let stand for 20 minutes before peeling and dicing. Mix with remaining ingredients and serve. *Serves 4*

Westway Salad Bowl

RAYMOND THOMAS, SR.

1 4-pound chicken	½ cup chives, chopped
Salt and pepper	3 hard-boiled eggs
1 medium-size avocado	1 cup French or Italian
1 large head lettuce, shredded	dressing
½ pound crisp-fried bacon	

Boil chicken in a pot with water to cover, seasoned with salt and pepper, until tender. Remove meat from bones and dice into bite-size chunks. Place in a large salad bowl. Add slices of avocado and shredded lettuce. Garnish with bacon, chives, and hard-boiled eggs. Add dressing and toss. *Serves 6*

Chicken Salad Theodore
RAYMOND THOMAS, SR.

3 breasts of chicken
½ cup Chicken Stock (p. 213),
 or salted water
1 head lettuce
1 stalk celery, chopped

4 tablespoons Mayonnaise
 (p. 244, or ready-made)
1 cup toasted almonds, chopped
Salt and pepper to taste
4 hard-boiled eggs

Poach chicken breasts in a little salted water or chicken stock until tender. Cool and dice chicken into cubes. Chop lettuce. Combine chicken with celery, mayonnaise, almonds, and salt and pepper. Place the lettuce in a large salad bowl and top with the chicken mixture. Garnish with the hard-boiled eggs. *Serves 4 to 6*

La Salade Vieux Carré
SHERMAN CRAYTON

1 head romaine
1 large handful fresh spinach
Dressing of choice

1 dozen spears cooked asparagus
1 dozen anchovies
3 hard-boiled eggs, sliced

Wash, tear up, and mix lettuce and fresh spinach. Add dressing of choice (French is suggested) and mix well. Decorate with asparagus and anchovies and top with egg slices. *Serves 4*

Sherried Bananas
CORINNE DUNBAR'S

6 half-ripe bananas, cut in
 half lengthwise
Shortening for frying
1 cup sugar
2 cups water

3 cloves
½ lemon, sliced
¼ cup butter
2 tablespoons sherry

Fry bananas in shortening until golden brown and remove from skillet. Brown the sugar in another skillet. Add water and cook until it forms a thick syrup. Add cloves. Add lemon, butter, and sherry and simmer 10 minutes. Add bananas and simmer 5 minutes. *Serves* 6

New Orleans or Louisiana Lemonade
AUSTIN LESLIE

6 lemons
5 tablespoons canned cherry juice
2 cups sugar
2-quart pitcher of water

Squeeze lemons and strain juice. Make sure seeds are removed. Put lemon juice in pitcher. Add cherry juice, sugar, and water. Shake or stir to mix. *Makes 6 8- to 10-ounce glasses; 12 glasses if crushed ice is used to fill glasses*

DESSERTS

Annie Laura's Coconut Lime Cake

ANNIE LAURA SQUALLS

2¼ cups sifted cake flour
1½ cups sugar
1 teaspoon salt
1 teaspoon baking soda
1 teaspoon baking powder
6 tablespoons butter

½ cup shortening
1½ teaspoons vanilla
1 cup buttermilk
4 egg whites (beat separately)
½ cup flaked toasted coconut

Preheat oven to 350°. In mixing bowl, sift together the dry ingredients. Add butter, shortening, vanilla, and buttermilk and blend. In separate bowl, beat egg whites until stiff. Fold into batter and beat 2 minutes more. Pour batter into 2 greased 9 x 1½-inch round cake pans. Bake for 25 to 30 minutes. Cool. Spread Lime Filling on one layer. Top with second layer. Frost with Fluffy Frosting and sprinkle with flaked toasted coconut.

Lime Filling

¾ cup sugar
2 tablespoons cornstarch
⅔ cup water
2 egg yolks
⅓ cup lime juice

1 teaspoon grated lime peel
2 tablespoons butter
1 drop green food coloring
  (optional)

In a saucepan, blend sugar and cornstarch. Gradually stir in water. Stir in slightly beaten egg yolks and lime juice. Cook while stirring over medium heat until mixture thickens. Remove from heat. Stir in grated lime, butter, and food coloring if desired. Cool.

Fluffy Frosting

1 cup sugar
⅓ cup water
¼ teaspoon cream of tartar

⅛ teaspoon salt
2 egg whites
1 teaspoon vanilla (pure)

Combine sugar, water, cream of tartar, and salt in saucepan and bring to a boil, stirring constantly until sugar dissolves. Place egg whites in mixing bowl (or smaller bowl if using electric mixer). Very slowly add the sugar-water mixture to the unbeaten egg whites, while constantly beating at high speed with electric beater until stiff peaks form. Stir in vanilla.

Pineapple Upside-Down Cake
ANNIE LAURA SQUALLS

¾ cup butter

⅔ cup granulated sugar

2 eggs, beaten

½ cup milk

2½ cups flour

4 teaspoons baking powder

1 teaspoon salt

¼ cup brown sugar

6 canned pineapple rings

Preheat oven to 350°. Cream ¼ cup of the butter and gradually add the granulated sugar. Add eggs and beat well, slowly adding the milk. Sift flour, baking powder, and salt and add slowly to the butter-sugar mixture, stirring constantly. Heat remaining butter and pour into cake pan. Sprinkle brown sugar over the butter and place pineapple slices on top. Pour cake batter carefully over pineapple. Bake for 50 minutes. Turn onto serving platter upside down. *Serves 8*

Deluxe Cream Cheese Cake
ANNIE LAURA SQUALLS

1½ cups sugar

6 ounces cream cheese, softened at room temperature

6 eggs

2 tablespoons orange rind, grated

3 tablespoons lemon rind, grated

Fine breadcrumbs, unsweetened

Preheat oven to 350°. With wire whip, mix sugar, cream cheese, eggs, orange rind, and lemon rind, in that order. Butter 2 9-inch-wide and 2-inch-deep cake pans. Sprinkle bottom of pans freely with breadcrumbs. Fill pans with cheese mixture. Place cake pans in a large baking pan containing an inch of water. Bake for 1½ hours. Remove from pan when ready to serve. Place 1 layer on top of the other. Add topping.

Topping

1 pint sour cream	1 cup halved fresh
2 teaspoons granulated sugar	strawberries or peeled,
1 teaspoon vanilla	sliced fresh peaches

Mix sour cream, sugar, and vanilla. Spread over cake and cover with fruit.

Gingerbread
ANNIE LAURA SQUALLS

½ cup shortening	2½ cups flour
1 cup molasses	2 teaspoons baking soda
½ cup sugar	2 teaspoons ginger
2 eggs	¼ teaspoon salt
½ cup boiling water	1 teaspoon cinnamon

Preheat oven to 325°. Beat shortening, molasses, sugar, and eggs together. Add boiling water. Sift dry ingredients and add to the mixture. Bake for 25 to 30 minutes in a square, greased baking pan. Serve with Brandy Sauce (p. 305), if desired. *Serves 8*

Flo's Coffee Cake
ANNIE LAURA SQUALLS

½ cup butter

1 cup sugar

1½ cups flour

1 teaspoon baking powder

2 eggs, beaten

½ cup milk

1 teaspoon vanilla

Preheat oven to 325°. Cream butter and sugar. Sift the dry ingredients. Add eggs and milk to the dry ingredients. Add vanilla. Pour in 9-inch greased and floured cake pan. Bake for 30 minutes.

Icing

¼ cup brown sugar

2 tablespoons butter

¼ cup cream

1 teaspoon vanilla

Pecans for topping

Mix all ingredients. Pour into double boiler and cook until butter and sugar melt. Spread on coffee cake and sprinkle with pecans.

Pie Crust
ANNIE LAURA SQUALLS

5 cups flour

⅛ teaspoon salt

1½ cups shortening

3 tablespoons ice water

Sift flour with salt. Put shortening in center of flour mixture and rub together with fingers until mixture becomes like corn meal. Add ice water. Form into ball. Roll out. Makes enough for top and bottom of a 9-inch pie pan.

Pecan Pie I
NATHANIEL BURTON

½ cup shortening
1½ cups flour
2 tablespoons water
½ cup brown sugar
1 tablespoon cornstarch

3 eggs, beaten
1 cup dark Karo syrup
1 cup light Karo syrup
2 tablespoons vanilla
1½ cups pecan pieces

Preheat oven to 350°. Mix shortening and flour. Add water, mix, cover, and let stand at least 30 minutes. Roll out and place in an 8-inch pie plate. In a mixing bowl blend sugar, cornstarch, and eggs. Add butter, both syrups, and vanilla. Mix thoroughly. Place pecans in bottom of pie plate. Add filling and bake for 40 minutes.

Pecan Pie II
ANNIE LAURA SQUALLS

3 eggs
1 cup light Karo syrup
3 tablespoons melted butter
1 teaspoon vanilla

⅛ teaspoon salt
1 cup pecan pieces
1 unbaked pie shell

Preheat oven to 325°. Beat eggs slightly. Add the syrup, butter, vanilla, and salt to the beaten eggs. Fold in the pecans and pour into unbaked pie shell. Bake for 30 to 35 minutes.

Lemon Chiffon Pie
NATHANIEL BURTON

4 egg yolks
1 cup sugar
2 tablespoons cornstarch
1 cup half-and-half
Rind of 1 lemon, grated

2 tablespoons powdered
   gelatin
¼ cup lemon juice
1½ cups heavy cream, whipped
1 baked pie shell

In mixing bowl, add egg yolks, sugar, and cornstarch. Blend well. Add half-and-half and lemon rind. Cook in double boiler. When mixture is hot, add gelatin. Continue to cook until mixture is as thick as whipped cream. Remove from stove and refrigerate until thick. Add lemon juice and whipped cream. Fill baked pie shell.

Rum Pie
ANNIE LAURA SQUALLS

2 tablespoons gelatin
½ cup water
1 cup sugar

6 egg yolks
½ cup dark rum
1 pint whipping cream

Mix gelatin and water in a saucepan and place over low heat for ten minutes. Remove from stove. Cream sugar and egg yolks and add to gelatin. Return mixture to heat for about 15 minutes. Remove from stove. Add rum. Cool. Whip the cream and fold into mixture. Pour into pie shell.

Graham Cracker Pie Shell
12 graham crackers
¼ cup sugar

3 tablespoons butter, softened

Crush graham crackers with rolling pin. Add sugar and butter. Mix together well. Press into pie plate to make shell. *Serves 8*

Cherry Pie
ANNIE LAURA SQUALLS

1 1-pound, 4-ounce can, or 2
  cups fresh pitted cherries
½ cup sugar
3 tablespoons cornstarch
3 tablespoons butter
1 tablespoon cinnamon
1 teaspoon nutmeg
Enough pie dough for top and
  bottom crusts (p. 296)

Preheat oven to 350°. Cook cherries over a low flame for about five minutes. If you are using fresh cherries, add about 1 cup water to start the juices cooking. Remove from stove and let cool for a few minutes. Add the rest of the ingredients. Return to low flame and cook for 10 minutes more. Pour into unbaked pie shell, top with crust, and bake for 45 minutes.

Apple Pie
ANNIE LAURA SQUALLS

4 cups chopped cooking
  apples
½ cup sugar
2 tablespoons cornstarch
1 teaspoon flour
1 teaspoon cinnamon
3 tablespoons butter
1 teaspoon vanilla
1 tablespoon lemon juice

Preheat oven to 350°. Mix apples with all dry ingredients. Add butter, vanilla, and lemon juice. Pour into a 9-inch unbaked pie shell. Add top crust and pinch edges together. Puncture center. Bake for 35 to 40 minutes.

Mirliton Pie
ROCHESTER ANDERSON

5 mirlitons
½ cup mirliton juice
4 egg yolks

½ teaspoon vanilla extract
1 can condensed milk
1 baked pie shell

Preheat oven to 350°. Cook mirlitons until soft, then peel, mash, and drain juice. Mix juice, eggs, and vanilla. Add mirlitons and milk. Cook slowly until thick, approximately 10 to 15 minutes. Cool and put in baked pie shell. Top with meringue and bake for about 10 minutes.

Meringue
4 egg whites
4 tablespoons confectioners' sugar

Mix egg whites and sugar and beat until stiff.

Ice Cream Pie
ANNIE LAURA SQUALLS

Pastry dough for 1 Pie Crust
  (p. 296)
½ pint chocolate ice cream
½ pint vanilla ice cream

½ pint strawberry (or pepper-
  mint) ice cream
8 whites of extra-large eggs
1 pound of confectioners' sugar

Preheat oven to 350°. Roll pie crust and place in 9-inch pie pan. Bake for 12 minutes. Cool. Spread ice cream in cooled pie shell in chocolate, vanilla, and strawberry sequence. Place in freezer for half an hour. Whip egg whites and confectioners' sugar together until it holds a peak. Remove ice cream pie from freezer and frost with egg white mixture, making sure to seal the sides. Bake

6 to 8 minutes at 450°. Cool and return to freezer. When serving, top with Chocolate Sauce (p. 305).

Apple Turnovers
ANNIE LAURA SQUALLS

1 Pie Crust recipe (p. 296)	2 tablespoons flour
2 tablespoons brown sugar	1 tablespoon cornstarch
3 tablespoons granulated sugar	1 cup coarsely chopped apples
2 tablespoons butter	Egg Wash (p. 107)
1 teaspoon lemon juice	Melted butter
1 tablespoon cinnamon	1 teaspoon granulated sugar

Preheat oven to 350°. Make up pastry recipe and roll out about ¼ inch thick. Mix all remaining ingredients, except egg wash, melted butter, and 1 teaspoon of granulated sugar, to make filling. Cut pastry into 5-inch squares and put 2 tablespoons of filling in each square. Fold over and press edges with a fork to seal. Puncture center of fold with fork. Coat with egg wash, brush with melted butter, and sprinkle with granulated sugar. Bake 20 to 25 minutes. Serve with hard sauce (see below). *Makes 8 turnovers*

Hard Sauce
1 tablespoon butter
1 cup confectioners' sugar
A taste of brandy

Mix all ingredients well.

Bread Pudding I
RAYMOND THOMAS, SR.

8 ounces (2 sticks) butter

3 egg yolks

½ pound sugar

2 cups milk

1 can evaporated milk

1 teaspoon vanilla extract

1 loaf French bread (stale)

1 fresh apple, diced

1 small can crushed pineapple

½ cup raisins

¼ cup light rum

Preheat oven to 350°. Beat 4 ounces (1 stick) melted butter, egg yolks, and sugar in bowl until smooth. Add whole and evaporated milk and vanilla and mix. In a separate baking pan, wet bread (avoid soaking), drain, and break up. Add fruit, 4 ounces (1 stick) of butter, and rum and mix. Fold egg-milk mixture into bread mixture in pan and bake for 1 hour (or until knife can be inserted into the mixture and comes out cleanly). *Serves* 4 *to* 6

Bread Pudding II
ANNIE LAURA SQUALLS

2 cups dry bread pieces

1 quart milk

3 eggs

¾ cup sugar

⅛ teaspoon salt

¼ teaspoon nutmeg

1 tablespoon vanilla extract

½ cup raisins

½ cup finely chopped apple

¼ cup butter

Preheat oven to 350°. Soak bread in milk until soft. Beat eggs until light in color. Add sugar, salt, nutmeg, vanilla, raisins, and apple. Mix with the bread. Dice butter and add to mixture. Pour in greased baking dish. Set baking dish in pan of hot water. Bake for about 1 hour. *Serves* 8

Bread Pudding with Whiskey Sauce
BON TON

1 loaf French bread	2 tablespoons vanilla extract
1 quart milk	1 cup raisins
3 eggs	3 tablespoons melted
2 cups sugar	margarine

Preheat oven to 350°. Soak bread in milk. Crush with hands to make sure milk is soaked through. Add eggs, sugar, vanilla, raisins, and stir well. Pour margarine in bottom of heavy 9 x 14 baking pan. Add bread mixture and bake till very firm, approximately 40 minutes. Cool the pudding, cube it, and put in individual dessert dishes. When ready to serve, add whiskey sauce and heat under broiler for a few minutes.

Whiskey Sauce

1 cup sugar	2 ounces bourbon whiskey, or
1 stick butter or margarine	to taste
1 egg, beaten	

Cream sugar and butter and cook in a double boiler until very hot and well dissolved. Add well-beaten egg and whip very fast so egg doesn't curdle. Cool and add whiskey. *Serves 8*

Bread Pudding with Rum Sauce
AUSTIN LESLIE

1 loaf stale French bread	¼ can evaporated milk
¼ pound butter	1¼ cups sugar
¼ pound raisins	1 small can crushed pineapple
3 eggs, beaten	3 tablespoons vanilla extract
¼ cup brown sugar	

Preheat oven to 350°. Wet the bread and squeeze the water out of it. Melt the butter and mix with all other ingredients. Pour mixture into a well-greased 4 x 10-inch baking pan. Bake for 2½ hours. The pudding will rise in the first hour. After an hour, remove pan from oven and stir the mixture to tighten it. Return to the oven for the second hour of cooking.

Rum Sauce
¼ stick butter, melted
1 cup flour
1 cup sugar
½ cup rum

Place all ingredients in double boiler and cook for 10 minutes. Beat until fluffy. *Serves* 10

Eggnog Bread Pudding
HENRY CARR

6 eggs
1 teaspoon nutmeg
1 teaspoon cinnamon
1 cup sugar
1 quart milk

1 tablespoon vanilla extract
½ cup raisins
½ cup canned pineapple chunks
6 slices of bread, cut into 4
    equal parts

Preheat oven to 350°. Break eggs into a bowl and add spices and sugar. Beat well. Heat milk and add to mixture. Add vanilla, raisins, and pineapple chunks. Stack bread, cottage style, in baking pan. Pour egg mixture on top. Bake for 1 hour. When cool, cut into serving pieces and pour rum sauce over each portion. *Serves* 8

Rum Sauce

1 cup milk

3 teaspoons cornstarch

½ cup sugar

2 ounces white rum

4 drops egg coloring

Allow milk to come to a boil. Mix cornstarch with cold water to make a loose paste. Pour into the milk and stir. Add sugar and rum and continue stirring until mixture thickens. Add coloring and mix well. *Makes 1½ cups*

Brandy Sauce
ANNIE LAURA SQUALLS

4 tablespoons flour

4 tablespoons sugar

5 tablespoons melted butter

4 cups milk, warm

3 eggs, well beaten

¼ cup brandy, or to taste

Add flour and sugar to melted butter and stir. Add warm milk and stir over low flame until mixture begins to thicken. Don't boil. Cool, then add beaten eggs. Heat for a few minutes over low flame. Add brandy. Can be served warm or cold. *Makes 5 cups*

Chocolate Sauce
ANNIE LAURA SQUALLS

1 quart heavy cream (or light cream, or half-and-half)

10 ounces unsweetened chocolate

10 ounces German sweet chocolate

1½ cups sugar

Mix cream, chocolates, and sugar together in a double boiler. Cook for 20 minutes. Remove from stove and let cool until ready to be used. *Makes 6 cups. Cut measurement in half for 3-cup yield.*

Cream Puffs
ANNIE LAURA SQUALLS

½ cup (4 ounces) butter   1 cup sifted flour
¼ teaspoon salt   4 eggs
1 cup water

Preheat oven to 375°. Combine butter, salt, and water in a saucepan. Cook over medium to low heat. Add flour all at once. Stir until a ball forms in center of the pan (from 3 to 5 minutes). Remove from stove. Add eggs one at a time, beating hard after each addition for about 2 or 3 minutes. Form into balls and bake for 15 to 20 minutes. When cool, fill with sweetened whipped cream. *Makes 8 cream puffs*

Danish Pastry
ANNIE LAURA SQUALLS

1 stick butter   1½ cups cake flour
½ cup sugar   3 tablespoons granulated yeast
¼ teaspoon salt   2 cups water
1 teaspoon vanilla extract   1 cup Glodo (see Glossary, p. 317)
3 eggs   ¼ cup dark Karo syrup
3 cups bread flour   ½ cup chopped pecans

Preheat oven to 350°. Cream butter, sugar, salt, vanilla, and eggs together. Stir together the flours and add butter mixture. Mix yeast and water in separate bowl to dissolve and let stand for a few minutes. Add yeast mixture to ingredients and mix. Take out of bowl and knead for a few minutes to remove air. Add Glodo. Fold over twice into a strip 6 inches long and 3 inches wide. Let stand in refrigerator for 7 hours. Flour table or board and roll out dough. Cut into squares and let rise for 20 to 25 minutes. Bake for 15 to 20 minutes. Brush with Karo syrup and sprinkle with chopped pecans. *Makes 24 squares*

Chocolate Soufflé

LOUIS EVANS

1¾ squares unsweetened
  chocolate
⅓ cup sugar
2 tablespoons hot water
2 tablespoons butter

2 tablespoons flour
¾ cup milk, scalded
Pinch of salt
3 eggs, separated
½ teaspoon vanilla extract

Preheat oven (see below). Melt the chocolate over hot but not boiling water. Add sugar and hot water and stir until smooth. In another pan, melt the butter. Add flour and gradually stir in the hot milk. Bring just to the boiling point, stirring constantly. Remove from the stove. Combine with the chocolate mixture. Add salt. Beat egg yolks until thick and add to chocolate mixture. Cool. Fold in stiffly beaten egg whites and flavor with vanilla. Pour into a baking dish and set in a pan of warm water. Bake 20 minutes in a moderate oven (375°) for a soufflé that is crusty on the edges with a soft center. For a firm soufflé, bake 40 minutes in a slow oven (325°). Serve as soon as taken from the oven, either plain or with whipped cream sweetened and flavored with vanilla. *Serves 3 to 4*

Strawberries Romanoff

LOUIS EVANS

2 cups fresh strawberries,
  sliced
2 ounces Cointreau

2 tablespoons sugar
1 pint whipping cream
1 pint vanilla ice cream

Marinate strawberries in 1 ounce of the Cointreau and sugar for 10 minutes. Whip the cream and combine with the ice cream and the remaining Cointreau in a bowl. Place strawberries in 6 serving dishes or glasses. A pastry bag is recommended for distributing the cream topping, which is piped over the strawberries. Top each serving with a sliced strawberry. *Serves* 6

Bananas Foster
NATHANIEL BURTON

1 cup brown sugar

1 stick butter

2 ripe bananas

3 ounces light rum

Vanilla ice cream

Put sugar and butter in chafing dish. Heat until sugar has melted. Peel bananas, slice lengthwise, then cut each section in half. Add banana pieces to sugar mixture. Cook approximately 3 minutes. Add rum. Cook 2 minutes longer. Put two banana quarters in each of 4 serving bowls. Top with vanilla ice cream. *Serves* 4

Cherries Jubilee
NATHANIEL BURTON

1 #303 can dark sweet cherries

2 ounces brandy

Vanilla ice cream

Put cherries in chafing dish. Bring juice to boil, then pour brandy over them and ignite. Put one scoop of vanilla ice cream into 6 dessert bowls. Pour cherries over ice cream and serve. *Serves* 6

Café Brûlot for Eight
CORINNE DUNBAR'S

Peel of 1 orange, sliced thin

4 sticks cinnamon

12 whole cloves

12 cubes sugar

6 ounces cognac

4 8-ounce cups of coffee

Place orange peel, cinnamon, cloves, and sugar in bowl. Pour cognac over it and ignite. Stir with ladle until sugar dissolves. Add coffee. Serve in brûlot or demitasse cups. *Serves* 8

Pure Coffee or Northern Coffee
NATHANIEL BURTON

4 tablespoons coffee
½ teaspoon salt
4 cups boiling water

Put coffee and salt in basket of a drip coffee maker. Add boiling water. Put top on pot and let drip. This coffee may be reheated over a low flame but should not boil. *Serves* 4

Coffee and Chicory or Creole Coffee
NATHANIEL BURTON

4 tablespoons coffee and chicory
½ teaspoon salt
5 cups boiling water

Put coffee and chicory and salt in basket of a drip coffee maker. Put top on pot and let drip. The coffee may be reheated over a low flame but should not boil, as it will become bitter. The best-tasting coffee is made in a drip pot rather than a percolator. *Serves* 4

LIST OF SUPPLIERS

[Editor's note: The list of suppliers has been retained from the original 1978 printing for historical reference. It should be noted that many of these suppliers are no longer in business.]

Some of the ingredients and cooking utensils mentioned in the text may be difficult to find in certain parts of the country. The list below constitutes the authors' suggestions of where certain items may be located in the New Orleans area.

GENERAL FOOD SUPPLIES:

filé; French bread; Glodo shortening; chili sauce; corn flour; fish fry; glace de viand; dried shrimp; Creole mustard; Creole horse-radish; pistachio syrup; Kitchen Bouquet

Gerde-Newman Company / 1300 S. Peters Street / New Orleans, La., 70116

Charles Dennery, Inc. / 698 St. George Avenue / Jefferson, La., 70121

Foltz Bros. / 633 Tchoupitoulas Street / New Orleans, La., 70130/ Spices and Herbs, only

MEAT PRODUCTS

Creole sausage; pickled pork; ham hocks; smoked ham

Chisesi Bros. / 2032 Lapeyrouse Street / New Orleans, La., 70116

L. Frank & Company / 1001 S. Broad Street /New Orleans, La., 70125

Imperial Meat Company, Inc. / 128 Airline Highway / Metairie, La., 70001

Thompson Packers, Inc. / 3259 Chippewa Street / New Orleans, La., 70115

FRESH PRODUCE:

mirlitons (chayotes or vegetable pears); tarragon leaves; wild chive; fresh thyme

R. Guerico & Sons / 200 N. Peters Street / New Orleans, La., 70116

SEAFOOD:

redfish; crayfish; shrimp with heads and tails intact; red snapper; crayfish fat

Battistella Seafood / 910 Touro Street / New Orleans, La., 70116

Ferrera Bros. Seafood / 729 Gov. Nicholls Street / New
Orleans, La., 70116

CREOLE COFFEE:

minimum order 1 crate (12 cans)

American Coffee Company / 800 Magazine Street / New
Orleans, La., 70130

Louzianne Coffee Company / 640 Magazine Street / New
Orleans, La., 70130

COOKING UTENSILS:

aluminum crab shells; papillote (parchment) bags; sautoires

Loubat Glassware and Cork Co. Ltd. / 510 Bienville Street / New
Orleans, La., 70130

GLOSSARY

Beef Base: beef-flavored granules (or powder) from which beef bouillon cubes are made. Available in most grocery stores.

Bouquet Garni: various seasonings tied into a small cheesecloth bag and dropped into soups, gumbos, etc.

Chicken Base: chicken-flavored granules (or powder) from which bouillon cubes are made. Available in most grocery stores.

Chicory: made from the root of the chicory plant. It is ground, roasted, and used as a supplement to or substitute for coffee. Louisiana-style coffee contains chicory and is readily available, both in that region and at specialty stores elsewhere.

Chili Sauce: a spicy tomato sauce, sweet and peppery.

Chinois Cap: a cone or "cap"-shaped sieve.

Clarified Butter or Drawn Butter: This is made by melting butter over very low heat. Skim off the white scum and strain the clear butter into another receptacle. Clarified butter is purer and does not burn as easily as unclarified.

Commercial Fish Fry: a combination of seasoned flour and meal especially prepared for frying or baking fish. Available in fish markets and grocery stores.

Corn Flour: not to be confused with corn meal. Corn flour is light and powdery; corn meal is grainy.

Crawfish: also known as crayfish. A small crustacean common in the Louisiana region. The meat resembles that of a lobster but is more tender.

Creole Mustard: a special, very hot mustard common to the Louisiana region. It is similar to a Dijon and frequently used interchangeably.

Creole Sausage or Creole Hot Sausage: a very hot and spicy sausage common to the Louisiana region. It is not to be confused with smoked sausage or "Polish" sausage, although in some cases either can be used as a substitute for Creole sausage.

Dried Shrimp: These have a very strong, concentrated shrimp flavor and should be used sparingly. Available in gourmet shops, Asian grocery stores, and many quality grocery stores.

Egg Wash: a mixture of eggs and milk in which certain meats, fish, or vegetables are dipped before frying or before dredging in flour or breadcrumbs and then frying.

Filé: dried and ground sassafras leaves, sometimes mixed with ground bay leaf. An indispensable ingredient of gumbos. Available in the seasonings sections of most quality grocery stores.

Glace de Viande: a meat extract available in most quality grocery stores. Can also be made by slowly reducing brown stock until thick and gelatinous.

Glaze: a sweet coating used to flavor certain foods (cakes and fowl especially) and make them attractive. It can be made with fruit juices or pulps mixed with sugar, vinegar, wines, etc. Marmalade and sherry; orange juice and brown sugar; jelly and wine are also often used.

Glodo: the brand name of a shortening. Available in Louisiana and a few other regions in the South. Other vegetable shortenings may be used in place.

Herbsainte: a liqueur with an anise or licorice flavor.

Oyster Water; Oyster Liquid: the liquid in the shell of a fresh oyster.

Papillote Bags: parchment paper shaped like a heart, made especially for baking. Ingredients are placed on top of a papillote sheet that has been oiled on both sides; the parchment is then folded into a bag and sealed. When the dish is ready to serve, the entire bag and its contents are put on a plate and the parchment slit down the middle. The food is eaten from the parchment.

Paw of Garlic or Garlic Paw: refers to the entire bulb of garlic, which is shaped like a small paw.

Pickled Pork; Pickled Rib Tips: pork marinated in vinegar. It is available in Louisiana, but seldom elsewhere. To make pickled pork, place chunks of fresh pork or pork ribs in vinegar and marinate overnight. Its flavor is distinctive and should not be confused with that of smoked pork.

Pickling Spice: a combination of herbs such as dill, rosemary, etc., readily available in the seasoning section of grocery stores.

Redfish: not to be confused with red snapper. Red snapper is red, and its meat is fine in texture. Redfish is a longer fish that can be identified by the black spot on its tail. It is generally less expensive than snapper. Both fish are best when they weigh between six and ten pounds, and are especially good stuffed or baked. They can be used interchangeably, although redfish is sweeter.

Rib of Celery or Celery Rib: a single stalk of celery.

Roux: a smooth paste made of flour and shortening or butter; the base of many sauces and gravies. Depending upon how long it is cooked, it can be a white roux, a golden roux, or a brown roux.

Smoke Flavoring: a seasoning with a smoky, charcoal taste. Found in the seasonings sections of most grocery stores.

Stock: the flavorful liquid made from the water in which meats, fish, vegetables, or fowl have been cooked. Recipes for stocks vary, but their use is not arbitrary; fish stocks, for example, should not be used with veal or pork. Rice can be cooked in either chicken or beef stock, depending upon the flavor desired and the food accompanying the rice. Stocks, other than fish stocks, are cooked at a simmer for a long time. They can be stored and used as base for a wide variety of sauces.

Tenderloin: used as a verb, e.g., to tenderloin a red snapper. To remove the skin and bones of a fish; to fillet.

INDEX